CAMPAIGN 275

RAMILLIES 1706

Marlborough's tactical masterpiece

MICHAEL MCNALLY

ILLUSTRATED BY SEÁN Ó'BRÓGÁIN
Series editor Marcus Cowper

First published in Great Britain in 2014 by Osprey Publishing,
PO Box 883, Oxford, OX1 9PL, UK
PO Box 3985, New York, NY 10185-3985, USA
E-mail: info@ospreypublishing.com
© 2014 Osprey Publishing Ltd

OSPREY PUBLISHING IS PART OF THE OSPREY GROUP.

ISBN: 978 1 78200 822 4
E-book ISBN: 978 1 78200 823 1
E-pub ISBN: 978 1 78200 824 8

Editorial by Ilios Publishing Ltd, Oxford, UK (www.iliospublishing.com)
Index by Alison Worthington
Typeset in Myriad Pro and Sabon
Maps by Bounford.com
3D bird's-eye view by The Black Spot
Battlescene illustrations by Seán Ó'Brógáin
Originated by PDQ Media, Bungay, UK
Printed in China through Worldprint Ltd.

14 15 16 17 18   10 9 8 7 6 5 4 3 2 1

AUTHOR'S NOTE

As always, I would like to express my gratitude to my wife, Petra, and our children – Stephen, Elena and Liam – for their patience and forbearance over the last year or so. Without their support and encouragement, I'd never have made it this far.

I'd also like to thank – and specifically dedicate this book to – Robert Hall and Iain Stanford, friends, authors and fellow students of 17th- and 18th-century warfare who have given unstintingly of their time to answer numerous questions and who have graciously given me access to their own collections to assist me in my research.

Finally a note on terminology – the forces commanded by Marlborough are commonly referred to as the 'Allied' or 'Anglo-Allied' Army, whilst those commanded by Villeroi and the Elector of Bavaria are usually referred to as the 'Franco-Bavarian' Army, a description that belies the significant number of Spanish or troops of other nationalities that stood in its ranks. Accordingly, and for brevity throughout the text, Marlborough's opponents will be referred to as either the 'Army of the Two Crowns' or the 'Bourbon Army'.

ARTIST'S NOTE

The artist would like to acknowledge the following people: the villagers of Ramillies, Offus, Autre Eglise, Marcus Cowper for his patience, Gabriele Mendella, Luc Vanlaethem, Pascale Bertrand, Au Temps des Cerises, Petra McNally, Robert Hall, Lemuel Black, Eric Timerije, Ralph Mitchard, Tomas O' Brogain, Maya Frost, Herminio Gomez and Roger Emmerson,
Readers may care to note that the original paintings from which the colour plates in this book were prepared are available for private sale. The Publishers retain all reproduction copyright whatsoever. All enquiries should be addressed to:

seanobrogain@yahoo.ie

The Publishers regret that they can enter into no correspondence upon this matter.

THE WOODLAND TRUST

Osprey Publishing are supporting the Woodland Trust, the UK's leading woodland conservation charity, by funding the dedication of trees.

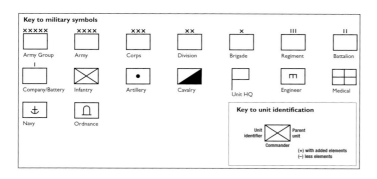

CONTENTS

Europe at the time of Ramillies

Legend:
- France
- Spanish Monarchy (inc. Balearic Islands, Milan, Naples, Netherlands, Sardinia, Sicily)
- Holy Roman Empire
- Denmark-Norway
- United Dutch Provinces
- Portugal
- Savoy-Piedmont
- Austria-Hungary (inc. Occupied Bavaria and the enclave around Barcelona)
- England (inc. Ireland, Scotland and enclave around Gibraltar)
- Neutral States (inc. Genoa (inc. Corsica), Mantua, Modena, Papal States, Parma, Swiss Confederation, Tuscany and Venice (inc. Dalmatia and the Morea)

Seas and water bodies: Baltic Sea, North Sea, Atlantic Ocean, Mediterranean Sea, English Channel

Rivers: Vistula, Danube, Elbe, Rhine, Meuse, Rhone, Seine, Loire, Thames, Tagus, Po

Cities: Stockholm, Warsaw, Copenhagen, Berlin, Dresden, Vienna, Buda, Pest, Hamburg, Munich, Venice, Mantua, Modena, Rome, Amsterdam, Cologne, Parma, Milan, Genoa, The Hague, Turin, Edinburgh, London, Paris, Versailles, Barcelona, Dublin, Bordeaux, Brest, Madrid, Gibraltar, Lisbon, Constantinople

THE STRATEGIC SITUATION

On the morning of 13 August 1704, an Allied army of around 52,000 men under John Churchill, Duke of Marlborough, met a slightly larger Franco-Bavarian force led by Camille, Duc d'Hostun – more commonly referred to by his secondary title as the Comte de Tallard – near the Bavarian town of Höchstädt. The previous year, a French army under Marshal Villars had crushed an Imperial army on this same ground and now, Tallard found himself unexpectedly in a position where he was unable to refuse battle, the result being a disaster for French arms that saw him a prisoner of war and his army in tatters. In the English-speaking world, the battle was named after Blindheim, the small village which saw the fiercest fighting and where the largest concentration of French troops was encircled and captured, and by its anglicized form – Blenheim – it is the name most synonymous with Marlborough's career.

In his recent account of the battle, the historian Charles Spencer refers to Blenheim as having 'stopped the French conquest of Europe', and yet whilst the 1704 campaign shows Marlborough at his best, not only as the possessor of a strategic sense that places him head and shoulders above his contemporaries but also as a battlefield commander of the highest ability, the battle did not stop the French military colossus dead in its tracks nor did it – as has also been argued – shatter the myth of French invincibility. This myth took a severe drubbing during the Italian campaign of 1701 when Prince Eugène of Savoy first overwhelmed a French force at Carpi in July and comprehensibly defeated a numerically superior Franco-Savoyard army under Villeroi at Chiari in September, before capturing this self-same officer at Cremona five months later.

The main effect of Blenheim was to remove, once and for all, the Bourbon threat to Vienna with the inherent possibility that, by thus knocking Austria-Hungary out of the war, France could militarily enforce the last will and testament of King Carlos II of Spain.

Throughout his final illness, King Carlos II of Spain was pressed by the various contending factions to alter his will in favour of their nominees. Under pressure from the Church, he bequeathed his kingdom to Philippe of Anjou, grandson of King Louis XIV, in the mistaken belief that all parties would accept his decision and the Spanish monarchy would remain intact. (Author's collection)

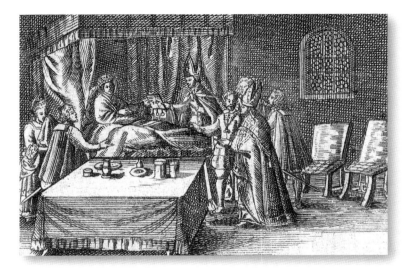

The king was a product of generations of extreme inbreeding, which had resulted in his developing a series of severe mental and physical disabilities. Both of his marriages had remained childless and, in an attempt to stave off the horrors of a disputed succession, his advisers needed to find an acceptable compromise heir outside the direct line of succession, as the two principal candidates – his cousins, King Louis XIV of France and the Holy Roman Emperor, Leopold – were the focal points of the Bourbon–Habsburg enmity that had divided Europe for the better part of the 17th century.

Naturally neither party could countenance the enrichment of his rival to his own detriment and, anxious to avoid another war, Louis began to open secret negotiations with the Maritime powers, England and the United Dutch Provinces, Austria's most prominent allies and two nations who already had their eyes on the expansion of their overseas trade at Spain's expense. After lengthy negotiation, it was agreed that the principal heir would be neither Louis nor Leopold, but Leopold's six-year-old grandson, Josef Ferdinand of Bavaria, whose claim was drawn through Maria-Antonia, the Emperor's only child with his late wife, Margaret Theresa, an elder sister of Carlos II, through his father's second marriage.

To sweeten the pill, it was agreed that the Bavarian prince would receive metropolitan Spain and the overseas colonies whilst the contentious parts of the European inheritance would be ceded to the nominees of Vienna and Versailles – the Spanish Netherlands would go to the Archduke Charles (Leopold's younger son through his second marriage) whilst the Italian territories – with the exclusion of the strategically important Duchy of Milan – would go to Louis's eldest son, and namesake, the Dauphin. Milan would be granted to the Duke of Lorraine, who would in turn cede his possessions of Lorraine and Bar to the Dauphin. On paper the treaty guaranteed European peace, but foundered jointly on Austrian demands that Milan should also go to the Archduke and the fact that Carlos would not countenance the dismemberment of the Spanish monarchy; he would instead acknowledge Josef Ferdinand as Prince of the Asturias, his sole heir.

Spain was torn between pro-French and pro-Austrian factions but nonetheless negotiations between France and the Maritime Powers continued, with an agreement being reached that would see Josef Ferdinand becoming King of Spain, with the Archduke Charles receiving the Duchy of Milan and the remaining Italian territories going to the Dauphin. Again, it looked as if an agreement had been brokered but, on 3 February 1699, whilst in Brussels to receive the support of the Flemish nobility, the six-year-old prince took ill and died. The succession would now be decided between the Habsburg and Bourbon candidates and, in the final year of his life, Carlos, in an attempt to secure the integrity of the Spanish Inheritance, nominated Louis's second grandson, Philippe of Anjou, as his sole heir, with the Archduke Charles being relegated to the position of third heir after Philippe's younger brother, Charles of Berry.

Still very much an evolutionary form of the more common 18th-century weapon, this French bayonet dating from the early 1700s fits over the muzzle and is affixed to the weapon by a lug, through the socket at the base of the weapon. Unlike later developments, which place the blade to the side of the muzzle, this curved blade fits around the muzzle and is effectively a direct extension of the musket itself. (Copyright and courtesy of Royal Armouries, Leeds)

For Louis XIV, the legacy was a poisoned chalice which presented him with two options, neither of which were particularly palatable to him: he could accept the will and repudiate the treaty, thus antagonizing Austria and the Maritime Powers, or he could remain bound by it, which would cause both an unnecessary break with Spain and an inevitable break with Vienna. Reasoning that further conflict with the Habsburgs was well-nigh unavoidable and would thus certainly bring the English and the Dutch into the ranks of his enemies, the French king decided to accept the will, proclaiming his grandson to be King Philip V of Spain by announcing: 'His birth called him to this crown. The Spanish People have willed it and demanded it of me: it was the command of heaven, and I have granted it with joy.'

Even now, war was not truly unavoidable. In London, the Tory administration was prepared to accept Louis's assurances that the French and Spanish crowns would never be united, and in any event was prepared to ignore the Partition Treaty on the grounds that it had been negotiated by King William III without reference either to his ministers or to Parliament.

War, however, did break out when Austria sent an army under Eugène into northern Italy with the intention of seizing the Duchy of Milan and presenting both France and her allies with a fait accompli. Naturally, Louis sent troops into the Duchy of Milan, ostensibly to safeguard the Spanish possessions, whilst still continuing to negotiate with the Maritime Powers. Initially Austria fought alone; however, escalation was inevitable as, upon the death of King James II, Louis openly acknowledged his son, James Francis Edward, as *de jure* King of England in opposition to both the English Act of Settlement (June 1701) and his own undertaking, in the 1697 Treaty of Ryswick to recognize William III as King of England. In consequence this brought Georg-Ludwig, Duke of Brunswick-Lüneburg – whose mother, the Dowager Duchess Sophia, was by virtue of the Act now third in succession to the throne of England – into opposition with France, whilst elsewhere in Germany, the Elector of Brandenburg was negotiating with Vienna over the possibility of his support during the current conflict, his price being the elevation of his Prussian possessions to the status of a 'kingdom'. This is not to say that the German states unilaterally supported the Holy Roman Emperor – the Electors of Bavaria and Liège–Cologne were members of the House of Wittelsbach, whose rivalry with the Habsburgs went back centuries and they saw an affinity with France as being the best way to gain ascendancy within the Empire, legitimizing their actions was the fact that Max II Emanuel of Bavaria was also Governor of the Spanish Netherlands and was thus obliged to uphold the late king's will; in addition, in order to destabilize the Empire, France

'The Pyrenees are no more!' Aware that acceptance of the Spanish Legacy would lead to almost certain warfare but conscious that its refusal would almost certainly lead to a lesser conflict with the bullish Habsburgs, Louis allowed his grandson to accept the Spanish Crown with the proviso that France and Spain would never be united under a single monarch. (Author's collection)

'The Dynast'. Given that his second son would not – in theory – inherit the Imperial title, the Emperor Leopold constantly pressed the lesser claim of the Archduke Charles to the Spanish throne. The Habsburg designs on northern Italy, and Leopold's refusal to compromise on what he held to be his son's rights, would effectively plunge Europe into 13 years of unnecessary warfare. (Author's collection)

agreed to support and subsidize any future Wittelsbach attempts to secure the Imperial throne. A number of other, smaller, German principalities also tended to support the succession of Philippe of Anjou, but these were ringed by Habsburg supporters and thus neutralized.

In May 1702, a joint declaration of war was issued upon France by England, the Holy Roman Empire and the United Dutch Provinces, which brought both the Maritime Powers and the body of the Imperial states into the war in support of Austria, a move which prompted the Wittelsbach brothers to declare openly for France. Accordingly, the Earl of Marlborough travelled to the Low Countries where he was appointed Deputy Captain-General of the Dutch forces, and became *de facto* commander-in-chief of the Allied Army.

After a failed attempt to bring the French Army of Flanders to battle at Zonhoven on 2 August, Marlborough began to concentrate on taking the enemy-held fortresses along the Meuse in order to protect the Dutch hinterland. On 22 September Venlo fell and, with Liège capitulating almost exactly a month later, Marlborough was now well placed to garrison the fortresses of Kaiserswerth, Roermond and Stevensweert, effectively driving a wedge between the enemy forces in Flanders and those on the Rhine.

In the other theatres, the Allies enjoyed mixed fortunes. Whilst the fighting in Italy remained inconclusive, the advantage gained by the capture of Landau by Ludwig of Baden on 2 September was negated by the Bavarian entry into the war on the side of France and, when Ludwig withdrew across the Rhine, he was narrowly defeated by the French at Friedlingen on 14 October. Elsewhere, an amphibious attack on the Spanish port of Cadiz was beaten off, although honour was somewhat restored when the English admiral, Sir George Rooke, destroyed the Spanish treasure fleet at the battle of Vigo Bay. In 1703, Marlborough successfully captured Bonn on 15 May, placing more pressure on the Franco-Bavarians, but was tantalizingly unable to capture the port of Antwerp at the mouth of the Scheldt, but the initiative passed to the enemy when Villars and Max Emanuel crushed an Imperial army under Styrum at Höchstädt on 30 September. The scale of the French victory was to show that it was not only Marlborough who had to deal with the delicacies of coalition warfare, for when Villars proposed that the Imperialists should be immediately pursued back to the gates of Vienna, a dispute with the Bavarian Elector ended with the marshal resigning his command and being replaced by the more pliable Marshal Marsin. The year ended on a military high but a political low for France with further victories over the Imperialists on the Rhine and Max Emanuel occupying the Tyrol in order to secure Bavaria's southern borders, whilst both Portugal and Savoy changed their allegiances and joined the Grand Alliance.

The French plan for 1704 was to detach a force of 70,000 men to upper Germany and from there to drive upon Vienna, thus knocking Austria out of the war and – despite much political rhetoric – enforce a settlement which would secure the Spanish throne for Philippe of Anjou. Versailles, however, had not reckoned with Marlborough's strategic insight and, with a combination of detailed planning and disinformation in the face of the very real threat to the Imperial capital, he led some 20,000 Allied troops southwards from the town of Bedburg, in order to unite with the armies of both Ludwig of Baden and Eugène, who had temporarily left the Italian front, before turning upon the Franco-Bavarian forces before they could attack the Habsburg capital.

The march to the Danube was a masterpiece of strategic planning in which Marlborough oversaw every aspect of the route, from the choosing of encampments to the establishment of forward magazines. It was a campaign of feint and counter-feint that left his opponents unsure of both his intent and destination, sowing the seeds of indecision that would allow him to unite successfully with the other Allied contingents. Having combined his forces with those of Baden, who was campaigning in Germany, the principal objective was to secure a bridgehead on the Danube which would not only serve as a base of operations and logistical hub, but would also facilitate the juncture with Eugène's forces coming up from the south-east, the final plan being that Eugène would screen Tallard's forces whilst Marlborough and Baden would engage the forces of Marsin and Max Emanuel.

The town selected for Marlborough's purpose was Donauwörth, where the bridge was overlooked by a fortified eminence, the Schellenberg, and as soon as the Franco-Bavarians became aware of the Allied plans, there followed a race to see who could occupy the town first, a race that the Allies lost, arriving before the town on 2 July. With the defences undergoing repairs and with the ramparts lined with enemy troops, Marlborough chose to forgo formal siege operations and elected to take the position by storm. Marlborough's first two assaults were bloodily repulsed by the enemy garrison, but a successful attack by Baden on a section of the fortifications that had by now been denuded of defenders was the precursor of a third assault that swept all before it. Although the Franco-Bavarian force had lost heavily (5,000 casualties with a further 3,000 or so taken prisoner) the Allied returns told their own story: out of some 22,000 men deployed for the attack,

LEFT
'The Master of all he surveys'. This 19th-century engraving of King Louis XIV of France manages to convey the monarch's hauteur but, despite this, he was more than willing to make a compromise settlement over the Spanish inheritance. (Author's collection)

RIGHT
'The Engineer'. Vauban's vision of a defensive grid, the *pré carré*, was to define the process of siege warfare for over four decades and would dictate the nature of the fighting in Flanders, much to Marlborough's despair and frustration. (Author's collection)

over 5,000 – including ten generals and 28 colonels, killed at the head of their men – became casualties, a level of attrition unprecedented in the conflict to date.

For the next month, the Allies devastated the Bavarian countryside in what was known as the 'rape of Bavaria' in an unsuccessful attempt to draw the Elector away from his loyalty to France, a process that was counterproductive as it placed undue stress on their own extended lines of supply and, as July turned to August, the two armies met to the north of Höchstädt in the battle that would bring Louis XIV's aims for 1704 to naught and lay the foundations of Marlborough's reputation as one of Britain's finest soldiers. With the battle won, and the threat to Vienna thus averted, the Duke began to lay his plans for the coming campaign season and as the army began to retrace its route northwards, he took steps to consolidate the Allied position in the Moselle Valley by capturing Trier and Trarbach, where he established magazines for the next year's campaign, with a third being set up at Koblenz, at the confluence of the Rhine and Moselle.

Late 19th-century German postcard showing detail of the uniform and equipment of a trooper in the Bavarian Cuirassier Regiment 'Arco'. (Author's collection)

From the moment of his arrival in Flanders, Marlborough had been beset by the problems of coalition warfare – not only did he have to contend with the differing personalities of the military commanders, but he also had to reconcile his strategic planning with the various allies' own diplomatic agendas; thus in the wake of the most comprehensive Allied victory of the war, he was about to propose a plan that would clearly be anathema to one important member of the coalition and simultaneously place an impossible strain on another. His plan for 1705 was intended to take the main theatre of operations away from Flanders, where strategic planning was constrained by the chains of fortresses, and instead launch an attack through Lorraine along what he called *le vrai chemain* – the true road. To modern readers, Marlborough's proposed attack will be reminiscent of the plans for the German attack on France in 1940, to render her defensive fortifications obsolete by bypassing them.

Boasting such fortified towns as Metz, Thionville and Verdun, the route was by no means undefended, and Marlborough's plan relied on three interlinked premises: firstly, that an Imperial army of 30,000 men under Ludwig of Baden would advance westwards from the fortress of Landau towards the river Saar, supporting his own army of 60,000 men marching from Trier; secondly, that the Dutch forces under Ouwerkerk would successfully contain the French Army of Flanders under Villeroi; and thirdly, that France and her allies would not be able to recoup fully the losses that they had suffered at Blenheim, the Schellenberg and their aftermath; therefore Louis and his generals would be faced with the alternative of diverting manpower to suitably garrison the fortresses lining his route or of deploying sufficient forces in the field to meet the Allies in open battle. He was confident of the likely outcome in either eventuality and when Vienna expressed concerns that the plan would lay Austria open to an attack by Marsin from Alsace, he simply pointed out that an Allied advance would either draw the French marshal westwards, or force him into dispersing his forces to cover several positions at once. In any event he would be unable to take offensive action.

The Allies' preparations throughout the winter had by no means gone unnoticed at Versailles and, as circumstance would have it, Louis was able to send perhaps the most talented of his commanders, the newly created Marshal Villars, who had been elevated after his victory at Friedlingen, to Lorraine, to take over the French forces there and organize its defence. This he did with vigour, and soon he was preparing a pre-emptive strike on the Allied magazine at Trier – which faltered because of adverse weather conditions – as well as a number of nuisance raids towards the Imperial camp at Landau. Believing that Marlborough would soon be attacking with almost 100,000 men, he decided that the best option would be to fortify a defensive position and invite attack. The French King was also politically receptive to the differences between the members of the enemy coalition and whilst he sent his finest general to take command of the threatened sector, he sent many of his best regiments, including Le Maison du Roi – his own household troops – to reinforce not only the Army of Flanders, but also the Dutch belief that the Spanish Netherlands would see France's main military effort in 1705.

Despite Marlborough's meticulous planning, the campaign was a disaster. Marching south from Maastricht, a number of Allied contingents had failed to join him and as a result he reached the area of operations with less than half of the number intended; next – and up on his arrival at Trier – he discovered that the magazines were less than half full; and finally the promised Imperial army failed to materialize. Couriers from Flanders brought messages of alarm from the Dutch Government, which naturally feared a French offensive, and the Duke sought to reassure the States General by promising that the success of his own campaign would force the enemy to return to the defensive in the north whilst they reacted to the threat from Lorraine. Fearing that a great opportunity would be lost if he abandoned his plan of operations, Marlborough elected to continue as planned.

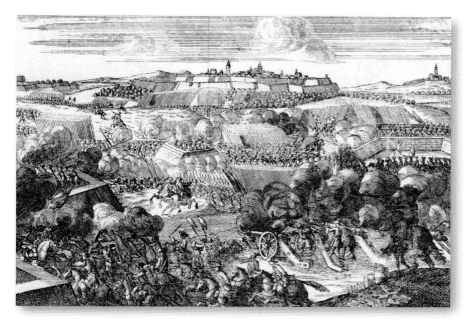

This contemporary print rather overplays Marlborough's 'breaking' of the Lines of Brabant during the summer of 1705. The works themselves were in no way as substantial as they are depicted here and the fighting was more in the nature of a heavy raid than a pitched battle. (Courtesy and copyright of la Bibliothèque Nationale de France)

A comrade-in-arms since their service together in the 1670s, Villars had a healthy respect for his opponent and took up a defensive position at Sierck, from where he would be able to cover the fortresses of Luxembourg, Saarlouis and Thionville, and where he could comfortably await reinforcement from Marsin in Alsace, which would increase his army to over 50,000 men. Believing reports that Marlborough's army was still larger than his own, Villars surrendered the initiative to his opponent, who daily looked eastwards for the reinforcement that would allow him to take the offensive, and gradually his command was swelled by the arrival of troops from Denmark, Prussia and the Palatinate but of the Imperial troops under Baden, there was still no sign.

With time and supplies both running out, and with Villars seemingly content to remain on the defensive and outwait his opponent, came the news that Marlborough wanted least of all – Villeroi had attacked Huy and the Dutch were now demanding that he immediately detach 30 battalions from his army to reinforce Ouwerkerk and forestall any French successes in Flanders. It was, naturally, the end of Marlborough's campaign. On 11 June, he wrote to Eugène, adamantly stating that the fault lay with the non-arrival of the Imperial reinforcements as – with those additional men – he would have been able to conduct offensive operations in Lorraine and, had he done so, the enemy would have been compelled to draw off troops from Flanders and thereby assuage Dutch concerns. Sickened by his allies' actions, he resolved to lead the army until the end of the campaigning season and then lay down his command in favour of a more suitable candidate.

The collapse of his planned campaign should have come as no surprise to Marlborough as, since having assumed command of the Allied forces in the Low Countries, he had seen ample evidence of the conflicting war aims of England's coalition partners. For the Dutch States General, the primary theatre of operations naturally remained Flanders and the Spanish Netherlands, the closest enemy concentration to their own borders, whilst for the Imperial princes, the main concern was focused on the Rhine frontier, whereas for the Austrian Habsburgs, their Imperial commitments notwithstanding, the only theatre of relevance, indeed the *raison d'être* for the war, was Northern Italy and the need to prevent it from falling into French hands. Priorities aside, then came the *style* of warfare: the Dutch preferred a slow and steady process consolidating their position through the prosecution of sieges and a gradual erosion of Vauban's defensive system. On the Rhine the situation was complicated by the personality of Ludwig of Baden, the

Victorian painting by Granville Baker showing the Duke of Marlborough leading the British cavalry against French infantry on the outskirts of Ramillies. Regrettably, in extolling Britain's military hero, the artist ignores the contribution of her allies. (Author's collection)

The Flanders campaign, June–August 1705

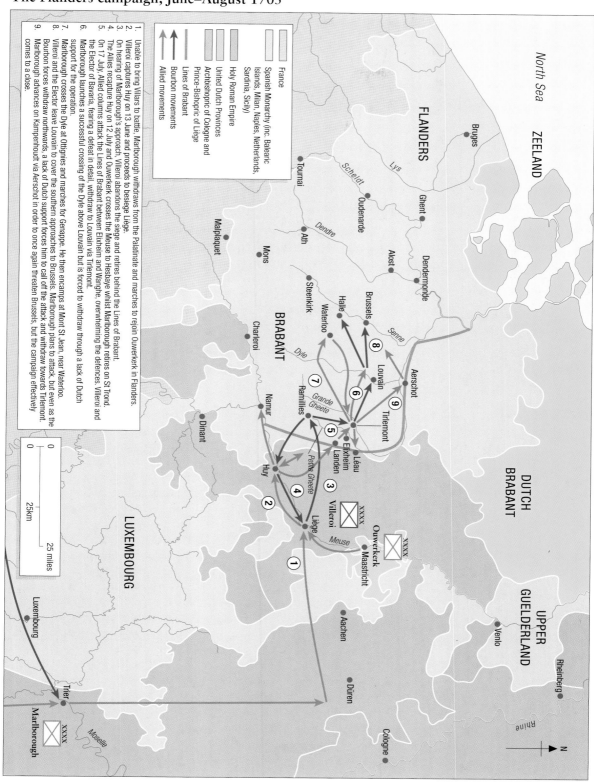

Legend:
- Allied movements
- Bourbon movements
- Lines of Brabant
- Prince-Bishopric of Liège
- Archbishopric of Cologne and
- Holy Roman Empire
- United Dutch Provinces
- Spanish Monarchy (inc. Balearic Islands, Milan, Naples, Netherlands, Sardinia, Sicily)
- France

1. Unable to bring Villars to battle, Marlborough withdraws from the Palatinate and marches to rejoin Ouwerkerk in Flanders.
2. Villeroi captures Huy on 13 June and proceeds to besiege Liège.
3. On hearing of Marlborough's approach, Villeroi abandons the siege and retires behind the Lines of Brabant.
4. The Allies recapture Huy on 12 July and Ouwerkerk crosses the Meuse to Hesbaye whilst Marlborough retires on St Trond.
5. On 17 July, Allied columns attack the Lines of Brabant between Elixheim and Wanghe, overwhelming the defences. Villeroi and the Elector of Bavaria, fearing a defeat in detail, withdraw to Louvain via Tirlemont.
6. Marlborough launches a successful crossing of the Dyle above Louvain but is forced to withdraw through a lack of Dutch support for the operation.
7. Marlborough crosses the Dyle at Ottignies and marches for Genappe. He then encamps at Mont St Jean, near Waterloo.
8. Villeroi and the Elector leave Louvain to cover the southern approaches to Brussels. Marlborough plans to attack, but even as the Bourbon forces withdraw northwards, a lack of Dutch support forces him to call off the attack and withdraw towards Tirlemont.
9. Marlborough advances on Kampenhoudt via Aerschot in order to once again threaten Brussels, but the campaign effectively comes to a close.

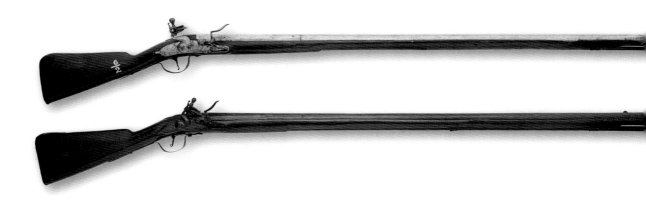

Imperial commander whose ego was seemingly greater than his desire for an Allied victory, whilst Eugène, the Austrian commander in Italy, remained closest to Marlborough's temperament and own strategic vision.

On 19 June, and having sent Hompesch ahead in order to advise Ouwerkerk of his intentions, Marlborough gave orders for the army to break camp and begin the long march north to Maastricht. The main body was left under the command of Charles Churchill, whilst the Duke himself rode ahead with the bulk of the cavalry, both columns to rendezvous at Düren, west of Cologne. In atrocious weather Marlborough pushed on and on the 21st he ordered his brother to send the Earl of Orkney with all of the remaining cavalry and a picked force of 10,000 foot to strike out for the rendezvous post-haste. Orkney and Marlborough arrived at Düren some hours apart on 25 June, the exhausted infantry standing proudly to attention as the Captain-General and the cavalry entered the town in their wake. The following day, whilst the mounted troops rested, and the remainder of the army made the rendezvous, Orkney led his column off once more to reinforce Ouwerkerk and assist in the relief of Liège.

Two days later the two wings of the army reunited and, at a council of war, with news coming from Alsace informing them that Villars and Marsin had joined their armies and thrown the Imperialist forces back from their defensive lines around Wissembourg on the Lauter, the two commanders agreed that the Germans would need to shift for themselves and that priority should be given to the recapture of Huy. On 4 July, with Ouwerkerk's troops moving to Vinaimont as a covering force, the town was invested and, with Villeroi remaining behind his own defensive works and allowing the siege to proceed unmolested, the garrison capitulated after eight days.

Still determined to lay down his baton at the end of the season, Marlborough began to plan an operation that would not only allow him to do so with his reputation intact, but also to leave the Allied Army in a better strategic position than would have ordinarily been the case. His plan called for a surprise attack on the French works near the Château of Wanghe on the Petite Gheete. Screened by extensive marshes, the defensive works were deemed impassable, but Marlborough's agents informed him of a stone bridge that the French had neglected to destroy. The position itself was defended by a small garrison and was sufficiently distant from its supports to convince Marlborough that it could be taken by surprise and a sufficient force transited to the French bank to dissuade any counter-attack.

After careful preparation, and a campaign of disinformation similar to that which had carried him to the Danube in 1704, Marlborough struck in the early hours of 18 July. Under the cover of darkness, a force of 20 battalions of foot and 38 cavalry squadrons overwhelmed the French position, and quickly formed up for action in preparation for the inevitable enemy response. The Allied commander – the Comte de Noyelles – did not have long to wait and although several French columns were converging upon his position, so was Marlborough, rushing up from the east with the rest of his forces. A general engagement ensued, one in which the Allies had the better of the fighting, and when the British cavalry routed the Bavarian squadrons opposing them, the Comte de Caraman – commanding the Bourbon forces – conducted a fighting withdrawal by forming his infantry into a hollow square and keeping the Allied horse at bay with regular and well-ordered volleys. Fearing that Villeroi and the Elector would be 'marching to the sound of the guns', Marlborough was content to let Caraman retreat unmolested.

The two Bourbon commanders had indeed gathered what troops they could but, coming within view of the battlefield and seeing the snaking columns of enemy troops moving toward Wanghe, they realized that the Allies could not be dislodged with the forces they had to hand. Although the French would play down the Allied success as a matter of 'no strategic importance', Marlborough had won his victory, gilded as it was, with the capture of five enemy generals, nine colonels and over 60 officers of other ranks, together with ten guns and nine Bavarian colours. It was perhaps the high point of a campaign which soon degenerated into a game of cat and mouse, in which Marlborough continually tried to manoeuvre Villeroi and the Elector into a position from which they would be forced to give battle, whilst those two worthies continually sought to elude the trap, relying on the passage of time and the end of the campaigning season to force the Allies into winter quarters and thereby relinquish many of the gains they had made since the Duke's return to Flanders.

And then came news that Marlborough had long dreaded – on 16 August, Vendôme had met Eugène in battle at Cassano, north-west of Milan, and although both armies had lost heavily, the battle had been a disaster for the Allies. Firstly, Anhalt-Dessau's Prussian corps had been decimated in the fighting and was no longer a cohesive formation but, perhaps more importantly, Eugène himself had been badly wounded during the fighting and had had to be withdrawn to Austria for medical treatment. Although Baden had been able to restore the situation in Alsace by late August, the defeat, coupled with the stalemate in Spain and unrest in both Hungary and occupied Bavaria, meant that the available resources needed to be carefully prioritized and, as such, Flanders was not viewed as a critical theatre of operations. Consequently, Marlborough would close the campaign knowing without a shadow of a doubt that his planned campaigning season would have brought the success he had intended and equally certain that, were he to remain in command of the Allied Army in the coming year, he would brook no political interference in his strategy.

Unable to force the enemy commanders into giving battle, and in conflict with many of his Dutch subordinates to whom his aggressive strategy was anathema, Marlborough withdrew towards Tirlemont and after dismantling a large section of the Lines of Brabant, the army continued to move eastwards, encouraging the enemy high command to believe that the failure of the Allies to engage was down to Marlborough's timidity rather than any action by his subordinates, and with the campaigning season drawing to a close, the Duke left the army under the command of Ouwerkerk and began a diplomatic tour culminating in a visit to Vienna.

At the Imperial Court, Marlborough took part in a series of conferences where he was able to persuade the Emperor to make concessions to the Hungarian rebels in order to redeploy forces to the field against the French. And then, perhaps most important of all, he was able to use his celebrity to secure a line of credit with a number of Austrian financiers so that Eugène would be able to resupply his army and be in a position to take the field in 1706.

From Vienna, Marlborough continued on to Berlin, where he renegotiated a treaty which would see further Prussian troops take the field in Northern Italy and then back to The Hague via Hannover. Throughout his journey, the Duke had – through a combination of compromise and conciliation – been able to paper over a number of cracks that had been appearing in the ranks of the Allies and as he returned to the Low Countries he felt that he now had sufficient support from his coalition partners to pursue what he knew was the right strategy to bring France to her knees and end the war.

During the spring of 1706, and sailing to London Marlborough received support for a plan by which he would leave the Dutch and Imperial troops to contain the enemy in Flanders and on the Rhine, whilst he would march to join Eugène with the remainder of the army and drive the Bourbon forces out of Northern Italy before invading Southern France.

Postcard showing a staff officer of the Bavarian regiment 'Kurfürst' c.1700. Coming under Maffei's command, the regiment fought in the southern sector of Ramillies village, but ultimately broke under pressure from the Dutch Gardes te Voet. (Author's collection)

Arriving back at The Hague on 24 April, he found that whilst the Dutch had become more conciliatory following correspondence with London, many of the allied princes had now begun to pursue their own agendas – the King of Denmark refused to allow his troops to leave their winter camps until their pay had been fully brought up to date, whilst the rulers of Hesse and Hannover would not allow their forces to serve in Italy whilst the King of Prussia was seemingly preparing to abandon the coalition.

Against this backdrop came the news that Vendôme had beaten the Imperialists at Calcinato on 19 April, and then on 1 May Marsin and Villars combined to attack Ludwig of Baden, driving him back across the Rhine and effectively putting Marlborough's planned junction with Eugène on hold and forcing the Duke to take the offensive in Flanders in order to regain the strategic initiative.

The Low Countries, spring to summer 1706

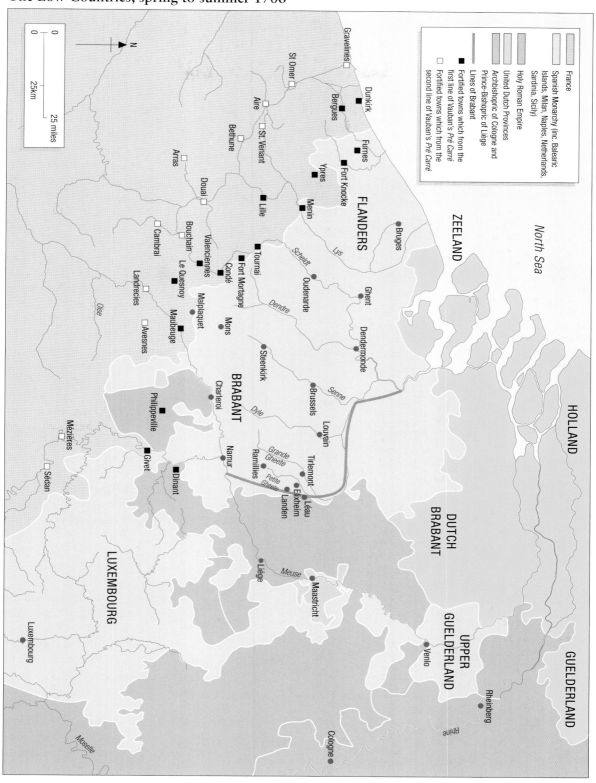

CHRONOLOGY

1700

March	William III of England and Louis XIV of France independently broker a partition treaty by which, upon the death of the King of Spain, Spain's empire will be split between the rival claimants to the throne.
25 August	The Emperor Leopold of Austria revokes his agreement to the Partition Treaty and demands that the Habsburg claimant receive the Spanish Empire *in toto*.
2 October	King Carlos II revises his will and, under pressure from both his Council of State and the Vatican, appoints Philippe of Anjou as his sole heir.
1 November	King Carlos II of Spain dies aged 39.
16 November	Philippe of Anjou acknowledged as king of Spain.

1701

February	England and the United Dutch Provinces officially recognize the Duc d'Anjou as King Philip V of Spain.
March	French troops march into the Spanish Netherlands and occupy the 'barrier fortresses', raising Anglo-Dutch concerns.
28 May	Austrian forces under Prince Eugène enter Northern Italy.
1 September	The French under Villeroi launch an unsuccessful attack on Eugène at Chiari.
7 September	Formal ratification of the 'Grand Alliance' between England, Austria, Brandenburg-Prussia and the United Dutch Provinces. The treaty will eventually expand to include Hanover, Portugal, Savoy and many of the minor German states.
16 September	Death of King James II of England.

1702

1 February	Eugène defeats and captures Villeroi at Cremona.
15 May	England declares war on France. Marlborough sent to command the Anglo-Dutch army in Flanders.
July	Imperial forces under Ludwig of Baden march into the Palatinate.
September	Ludwig of Baden forced to raise the siege of Landau. Bavaria enters the war as an ally of France.
12 October	Sir George Rooke captures the Spanish treasure fleet in Vigo Bay.
14 October	Ludwig of Baden defeated at the battle of Friedlingen.

1703

May	Marlborough captures Bonn, but is unable to exploit victory. French army under Villars joins Max II Emanuel of Bavaria.
13 July	Villars defeats Ludwig of Baden at Munderkingen.
19 September	Villars defeats Hermann von Limburg-Styrum at Höchstädt.
October	Max II Emanuel of Bavaria cancels Villars's proposed attack on Vienna. Villars resigns his commission and is replaced by Marsin.
25 October	Duke of Savoy repudiates alliance with France and joins the Allies.

1704

February	Archduke Charles lands in Portugal to press his claim to the throne of Spain.
July	Marlborough marches to Bavaria to counter the threat to Vienna. Marlborough victorious at the Schellenberg and Donauwörth.
23–24 July	British forces capture Gibraltar.
13 August	Marlborough and Eugène victorious at Blenheim (2nd Höchstädt). Anglo-Dutch fleet victorious at the battle of Vélez-Malaga. Bourbon Spanish troops besiege Gibraltar. Max II Emanuel flees to the Spanish Netherlands where he is appointed governor by King Philip V. Bavaria occupied by Imperial forces.

1705

March	Anglo-Dutch fleet victorious at the battle of Marbella. Bourbon forces abandon the siege of Gibraltar.
June	Allied forces land in Catalonia.
October	Allies capture Barcelona.
November	Bourbon forces besiege Barcelona.

1706

April	Marshal Vendôme defeats an Imperialist army at Calcinato in Northern Italy.
23 May	Marlborough decisively defeats Villeroi at Ramillies.
September	Eugène breaks Bourbon siege of Turin and relieves city.

OPPOSING COMMANDERS

THE ALLIED ARMY

John Churchill, 1st Duke of Marlborough (1650–1722)

A senior officer under both King Charles II and his successor James II, Churchill's star continued to wax in the wake of the Glorious Revolution and, in the coronation honours, he was created Earl of Marlborough. Whilst his King led a primarily 'continental' army against the Jacobites in Ireland, the newly elevated peer assumed command of an English contingent dispatched to fight in the Low Countries where he served with distinction.

Following the battle of the Boyne, and William's subsequent inability to end the war with the capture of the stronghold of Limerick, Marlborough devised a plan to secure the southern coast of Ireland and thus sever Jacobite links with France. The plan was an outstanding success and was a demonstration of his grasp of both logistics and the need for allied commanders to be able to work together both in the field and at higher levels. Needless to say, Marlborough's rise to pre-eminence within the army and the fact that he was the former king's brother-in-law soon led to increased tension between King William and his general, strains that were only exacerbated by what many believed were his traitorous communications with his relatives at the Jacobite court in exile.

The outbreak of the War of the Spanish Succession and the need for the commitment of English troops to the Allied armies meant that, following Anne's accession in 1702, Marlborough was appointed Captain-General of the army and led the English contingent to Flanders, where he soon received an appointment to command the Anglo-Dutch forces, his English title being raised to that of duke.

A combination of French strategy and dissent within the ranks of his nominal subordinates meant that Marlborough's plans for 1703 met with limited success, but even then he was planning the feat that would write his name in

'The Captain-General'. It was Marlborough's determination to break out of the rut of previous campaigns that led him to seek out Villeroi's army in a decisive engagement that would eventually alter the whole conduct of the war in Flanders. (Author's collection)

the history books, the march to the Danube in the summer of 1704 in order to relieve enemy pressure on the Imperial capital – Vienna – and which would see him secure his first major victory at Blenheim on 13 August.

The seal should have been set on a successful follow-up campaign in 1705 but when Marlborough advanced into Alsace, he found that Villars, the French commander, was unwilling to offer battle and remained behind his entrenchments. At the end of his supply lines and unable to remain in the field much longer, Marlborough returned with his troops to Flanders and, breaking the French siege of Liège, he combined with the Dutch under Ouwerkerk to break through the French Lines of Brabant near Elixem, but was again thwarted from developing his offensive fully by a number of Dutch officers who believed that he was deliberately sacrificing Dutch troops to secure his objectives.

For Marlborough it was another salutary lesson in the prosecution of coalition warfare, and one that he vowed to learn from. For 1706 he would set himself two simple objectives: firstly, to meet and destroy the enemy army in the field, wherever it would be found and then, a distant second, to define any additional or political objectives.

Hendrik Van Nassau, Heer Van Nassau-Ouwerkerk (1640–1708)

A grandson of the Dutch general Maurice van Nassau, Ouwerkerk first entered service as equerry to his second cousin, Prince William-Henry (later King William III) at the age of 26 and fought under the prince's command throughout the Franco-Dutch War (1672–78), distinguishing himself at both Seneffe (1674) and St Denis (1678), where he saved his sovereign's life. As a result of his service during the conflict, he was elevated to the nobility of Utrecht by the States General and created an Imperial count by Leopold I in 1679.

A member of William's personal entourage, he accompanied him on the expedition to England in November 1688 and became a naturalized citizen the following year, at which time he was made the King's chief equerry and he would no doubt have come into close and regular contact with the Earl of Marlborough, his future commander. Appointed to command the Stadtholder's Horse Guards, he led them into action at Neerwinden in July 1693 and thereafter served in Flanders under the command of the Prince de Vaudémont.

In 1696 Ouwerkerk was promoted to major-general on the English establishment, and promoted to lieutenant-general the following year, finally becoming General of Horse in 1699. In 1701, he was given the honorary rank of general on the Dutch establishment, and two years later was appointed Field Marshal of the States army.

The senior Dutch officer under Marlborough's command, Ouwerkerk's service – whilst unspectacular – proved to be exactly what was required in a delicate politico-military situation. Firstly he was a competent officer, a capable pair of hands, whom Marlborough could trust implicitly to operate within the scope of his orders;

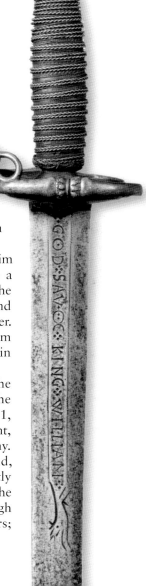

Many weapons, such as this cavalryman's sword dating from the late 17th to early 18th century, were often inscribed with loyal mottos or exclamations. This example requests divine protection for (the then King) William III, predecessor of Marlborough's patron, Queen Anne. (Copyright and courtesy of the Royal Armouries, Leeds)

secondly he was a perfect foil for those officers who were overtly vocal in their criticism of the English Captain-General; and thirdly and finally, as a member of the House of Nassau, he was a perfect conduit to the Dutch Government. These qualities can be fully seen in his operations in Flanders during 1704 when he commanded those troops left in theatre after Marlborough's march to the Danube, and then the following year when he screened the province during the abortive campaign in Alsace. They can also be seen later when the two commands had reunited and he commanded one wing of the army, which broke through the Lines of Brabant and then – unsuccessfully – tried to bring the Bourbon forces under Villeroi to battle.

Charles Churchill (1656–1714)

Like his more famous elder sibling, Charles Churchill began his service at Court as a result of the influence of his eldest sister Arabella, who was mistress to James, Duke of York. Appointed page of honour to King Christian V of Denmark upon his accession in 1670, he eventually became gentleman of the bedchamber to the king's brother, George, who was to be the future husband of the Princess (later Queen) Anne. After the Glorious Revolution Churchill joined the army, no doubt benefiting from the patronage of his brother, recently created Earl of Marlborough, and serving under his command in Ireland in 1690.

Three years later, and by this time a brigadier, Churchill fought at the battle of Landen in 1693, where he had the luck to capture his nephew James, Duke of Berwick, who was one of the enemy commanders. The following year he was promoted to Major-General of Foot, and was appointed as Governor of Kinsale. His continued able and loyal service was rewarded in May 1702 when he received his promotion to lieutenant-general. By this time he had become, by dint of hard work, one of Marlborough's most able and trusted subordinates and at Blenheim (13 August 1704) he led the British troops that, secured the passage of the Nebel and captured the village of Blindheim, a feat that saw him rewarded with the Lieutenancy of the Tower of London. At Ramillies he would direct the Allied centre, conducting the attacks on both Ramillies and Offus, eventually breaking the enemy main battle line when its right flank was turned by Ouwerkerk's reinforced cavalry wing.

George Hamilton, 1st Earl of Orkney (1666–1737)

The fifth son of William Douglas, 1st Earl of Selkirk, Hamilton joined the army in May 1684, being commissioned as a captain in the Royal (Scots) Regiment of Foot, commanded by his uncle George Douglas, Earl of Dumbarton. During the Glorious Revolution, Lord George followed his father's lead and faithfully supported William of Orange, serving in Ireland, where on 1 March 1690 he assumed command of Thomas Lloyd's regiment of Enniskillen foot, leading the unit at the Boyne, Aughrim and the sieges of Athlone and Limerick. In 1692, Hamilton's regiment was disbanded and he transferred to the Royal Fusiliers but on 1 August, he assumed the colonelcy of the Royal Scots, just in time to lead it into action at Steenkirk. Over the next few years, Hamilton saw extensive service in the Low Countries, again serving with distinction at Landen in 1693, and was promoted to brigadier on 1 July 1695, just as the Allies commenced with the investment of Namur. Badly wounded during the siege, he returned to England to convalesce and three months later married Elizabeth, daughter of Edward Villiers, Earl of Jersey, and in January 1696 was then himself raised to the Scottish peerage as Earl of Orkney, Viscount Kirkwall and Baron Dechmont.

'The Warrior'. George Hamilton, Earl of Orkney. Irrespective of whether one accepts the suggestion that his attack was an elaborate feint or not, Orkney's initial movement fixated the Bourbon commanders to such an extent that the tactical initiative remained firmly in Marlborough's hands. (Author's collection)

Further promotion came on 3 March 1702 when Orkney became a major-general, and on 1 January 1704 when he received his promotion to lieutenant-general, with the rare distinction of having taken part in every major engagement in which British troops were present from the Boyne through to Ramillies. Furthermore, during the War of the Spanish Succession, it could be said that he rose to the height of his military skills at Blenheim in August 1704. Orkney led the attack that would eventually secure the village of Blindheim and ultimately victory for the Allies, whilst the following year his dash led to the relief of the citadel of Liège which the Bourbon forces had besieged during Marlborough's absence in Alsace.

By now one of the Captain-General's most trusted subordinates, his capable handling of the Allied right wing at Ramillies ensured that Marlborough's ambitious battle plan would be successfully realized.

THE ARMY OF THE TWO CROWNS

François de Neufville, 2nd Duc de Villeroi (1644–1730)

The son of Louis XIV's childhood governor, Villeroi grew up as part of the future King's inner circle and thus his future at the Royal Court was more than assured. Like many of his peers, the young nobleman fought as a volunteer in the Imperial armies against the Turks, and was wounded at the battle of St Gotthard in 1664. Returning to France, he was appointed colonel of the 'Lyonnais' regiment of foot and, three years later, when the King campaigned in Flanders at the head of his armies, Villeroi was there as well, taking part in the sieges of Douai, Tournai and Lille. In 1673 he transferred to Alsace where he served under Turenne, and may have come to know Colonel John Churchill, an English officer similarly serving under Turenne's command.

More a courtier than a soldier, Villeroi's military career was punctuated by the unfortunate distinction of his being defeated by both Eugène (Cremona, 1702) and Marlborough (Ramillies, 1706). (Author's collection)

The following year and newly promoted to *maréchal de camp* he returned to the western theatre, taking part in the conquest of the Franche-Comté and distinguishing himself at the sieges of Bouchain and Condé, for which he was promoted to lieutenant-general and inducted into the Order of St Louis.

In 1692, during the War of the League of Augsburg, Villeroi distinguished himself at both the battle of Steenkirk and the siege of Namur, being made a Marshal of France, and a Chévalier of the Order of St Louis, commanding the French forces which captured both Huy and Charleroi the following year. When the Marshal Duc de Luxembourg – one of France's finest generals, and the commander of the Army of Flanders – died in 1695, it was Villeroi's standing at Court rather than any inherent military ability that secured him the army command.

Subservient at Court, Villeroi began to demonstrate his natural hauteur in 1701 when he was sent to command the French forces in northern Italy and went out of his way to remind the Duke of Savoy that his position was more that of a French subordinate than a sovereign ruler. The disastrous attack on Eugène at Chiari on 11 September 1701 was made at Villeroi's insistence and, whilst his subordinate, Marshal Catinat, was summoned to Versailles to answer for his conduct during the battle, Villeroi remained undisturbed at his Italian headquarters. It was a peaceful interlude that was not destined to last long as, several months later, Eugène launched a surprise raid upon the French positions at Cremona and, whilst the Imperial forces were beaten back, the French marshal was taken, spending the next two years as a captive until he was exchanged in 1704.

Upon repatriation, Villeroi reassumed command of the Army of Flanders, and his relative success in staving off defeat during the next two years was more due to political divisions within the Allied command structure than to any innate military skill. When the 1706 campaigning season opened, Villeroi mistakenly pursued an aggressive strategy, whereas a more passive approach might have stifled Marlborough's tactical ability whilst other – more able – commanders, such as Villars or Vendôme might have been able to secure the victory France needed in order to compel the Allies to the negotiating table.

In the aftermath of Ramillies, Villeroi's performance was heavily criticized by both a number of his battlefield subordinates as well as by a coterie of influential courtiers at Versailles, a critique that was endorsed by his own willingness to accept rather than to apportion blame. On his return to Versailles, his childhood friend took him to one side, saying, 'At our age, one is no longer lucky' and with that, the Marshal de Villeroi was removed from the command of the Army of Flanders, to be replaced by the Duc de Vendôme who had earlier replaced him in Italy. He would never again hold military command.

Maximilian II Emanuel, Elector of Bavaria (1662–1726)

Having ascended to the Electoral throne as a minor in 1679, and anxious at French expansionism, Max Emanuel lost no time in overturning the Francophile policies of his guardian and uncle, Philipp von Leuchtenburg, that saw a rapprochement with Austria in the form of both political and military treaties and, when an army was raised to relieve the Ottoman siege of Vienna in 1683, the Elector led the 11,000-strong Bavarian contingent in person.

After the relief, Max Emanuel remained in Imperial service, becoming known to the Turks as the Mavi Kral or the 'Blue King' from the colour of his tunic that stood out clearly amongst the ranks of their enemies, with the Bavarian forces taking part in the capture of Esztergom and the unsuccessful assault on Buda the following year. As a result, the Emperor Leopold saw the dashing Elector as an important ally within the Imperial states and offered him the hand of his daughter, the Archduchess Maria Antonia in marriage, through which union his heirs would have a claim on the Spanish throne.

In 1686, during the continuing campaign against the Turks, Max Emanuel led – and was wounded during – the successful assault on Buda. The following year, he held joint command (with Ludwig of Baden) of the Imperialist right wing at Mohács and, following a dispute with Charles of Lorraine, the Imperial commander-in-chief, he began to agitate to be given the position himself, threatening a dissolution of the Austro-Bavarian alliance should his demands not be met. Leopold conceded to his son-in-law, who led the Imperial forces to a number of victories, notably the capture of Belgrade, but Max Emanuel was becoming disillusioned with his father-in-law whose substantial promises were never backed up by his actions and it became clear that Bavaria was bankrupting itself whilst fighting Austria's wars.

During the Nine Years War, Max Emanuel fought once again on behalf of Austria, but this time it was in the Rhineland against the armies of France and in 1691 his further loyalty was rewarded when he was made Governor of the Spanish Netherlands. This turned out to be another drain on the Bavarian treasury, but one that would be borne whilst the Elector's son Josef Ferdinand remained heir to the Spanish monarchy.

'The Image of the Ideal Soldier'. This 20th-century postcard shows the Elector Max Emanuel charging into action at the head of the Kürassier regiment 'Weickel'. At Ramillies the regiment deployed on the rising ground between Autre-Église and Offus. (Author's collection)

Relations between Munich and Vienna began to grow more distant with the death of Maria Antonia in 1692, and then more so two years later when the dynastically ambitious Elector married Theresa Kunigunda, daughter of King John III 'Sobieski' of Poland. Ties between the two countries broke at the turn of the century with the death of Prince Josef Ferdinand and the devolution of the Spanish succession into a Bourbon–Habsburg competition.

It was now that Max Emanuel began to harbour ambitions for his family, the Wittelsbachs, to supplant the Habsburgs on the Imperial throne and when the War of the Spanish Succession broke out in 1701, he allowed French forces to occupy a number of fortresses in the Spanish Netherlands. Upon his return to Bavaria he unsuccessfully agitated for the Empire to remain neutral in any conflict over the Spanish throne.

Bavaria entered the War of the Spanish Succession in mid-1702 as an ally of France, her presence offsetting a number of Imperial successes in the Rhineland but, the following year and despite the assistance of French troops, a Bavarian occupation of the Tyrol in 1703 was a complete debacle. Undeterred Max Emanuel ignored calls for him to negotiate with Austria and continued with his campaign, by the year's end capturing the city of Augsburg which was followed by Passau early in 1704. Despite this, peace talks began but faltered when Max Emanuel demanded royal status within Bavaria, similar to that which had been granted to Friedrich III of Prussia in 1701. As a result, Bavaria entered into a formal alliance with France and a combined army began a drive to capture Vienna and force Austria to come to a negotiated settlement.

The campaign met with total disaster at Blenheim on 13 August, when the Franco-Bavarians were soundly defeated by an allied army under the Duke of Marlborough. Max Emanuel left his homeland and, relying on his allies' goodwill, effectively went into exile for the rest of the war, serving with the Bourbon armies in Flanders.

The presence of the Allied siege trains with Marlborough's field army not only gave him a significant numerical superiority in artillery, but the howitzers and heavy-calibre weapons caused havoc amongst the Bourbon defensive works. (Photograph courtesy Iain Stanford)

OPPOSING FORCES

THE ALLIED ARMY

Throughout his service in Germany and the Low Countries, Marlborough was in an unenviable position that has possibly never – at least not to the same degree – faced a British officer in the field. Firstly he had to maintain a coalition in which the various parties each had their own political and military objectives, which they would pursue above all considerations, and, secondly, within his own theatre of operations he had to create an army, not only out of the enlisted troops of several states, but also those contingents that had been contracted in order to make up shortfalls in manpower. Each of these latter formations had its own individual contract of employment that would cover aspects such as pay, compensation for casualties, etc, creating anomalies such as the upkeep for certain units within the Danish contingent being paid for by the British Government and others being paid for by the Dutch Government, a situation which not only led to excessive bureaucracy but could also lead to tensions within the high command.

Luckily for the Duke, he was supported by an able team of subordinates, first of whom was William Cadogan, his Quartermaster General, as well as a number of senior officers who had served with Marlborough for several years. Foremost amongst these were the Dutch Field Marshal van Ouwerkerk, who also held the rank of General of Horse on the English establishment and who had been one of Marlborough's peers during the reign of King William III, and of course Charles Churchill, his younger brother, who was the senior infantry commander. Both men were crucial to the running of the army, not just in military terms, but also – and especially in the case of Ouwerkerk – as a conduit to the Dutch Government, by which the political concerns of the States General could be assuaged.

The army itself was a truly multinational force consisting of 74 battalions of foot – roughly 50,000 men – drawn both by enlistment and also by contract from several countries, each with an average strength of around 500 men organized into ten or so companies, armed with a smoothbore musket and socket bayonet. In the main, most of the infantry were trained to give fire by platoon, which meant that they would deliver rolling volleys one section at a time, the main advantage of this drill being psychological, keeping the enemy under continual fire, rather than any massive increase in casualties caused to the enemy.

The mounted wing comprised 123 squadrons, accounting for something in the region of 20,000 men who, unlike their counterparts within the Bourbon forces, were trained and indeed encouraged, to fight in the mounted role rather than being differentiated between 'horse', the heavy cavalry of the line, and 'dragoons', who were effectively mounted infantry whose main function was to seize and hold terrain or support an infantry attack. As such, the Allied cavalry would ultimately gain an advantage over the enemy, which would be in excess of the near parity in number. However, it was an advantage that would be evidenced only once Marlborough had developed his attack to the degree whereby he was able to transfer two cavalry brigades from his relatively unengaged right flank in order to support Ouwerkerk's attack on the left which had stalled against the Bourbon right flank to the south of Ramillies.

Finally, we come to the Allied artillery, which gives an insight into Marlborough's tactical and strategic planning in May 1706. Firstly, the presence of the Dutch siege train with the army confirms that the Duke's plan of campaign was to rely on speed – with the heavy artillery 'at the front' he would be able to develop any victory into an assault on either Brussels, Louvain or Namur, the capture of any of which would then allow him to maintain the strategic initiative and break out of the rut of the previous years' campaigns. As such, he elected to deploy these guns with great effect against the Bourbon defences of Ramillies, whilst the heavier field pieces were used in batteries against the enemy battle lines, and the lighter were dispersed amongst the various infantry brigades for individual close support, as evidenced by the two cannon which were attached to Werdmüller's ad hoc command in the Mehaigne Valley.

THE ARMY OF THE TWO CROWNS

Villeroi took the field in May 1706 under a great misapprehension – with his two, more able colleagues Villars and Vendôme commanding in Germany and northern Italy respectively, all he really needed to do was to contain Marlborough, in effect, simply not be defeated.

Like its opponents, the Army of the Two Crowns was also a multinational force – at its core was Villeroi's (French) Army of Flanders, to which was added the army's Spanish counterpart as well as a number of German expatriate forces from the Elector of Bavaria and his brother the Prince-Bishop of Cologne, who had supported King Louis XIV against the Holy Roman Empire, and who were both in exile, the former as Vicar of the Spanish Netherlands, and the latter as a French pensionary.

The army, however, was nowhere near as numerous as that which the Allies could put into the field and so, whilst petitioning Versailles for reinforcement from Marshal Marsin in Lorraine – some 20 squadrons of Marsin's cavalry would arrive in time to participate in the battle, with the infantry following in their wake – Villeroi made the unfortunate decision to strip the garrisons from a number of Spanish fortresses and use these units to augment his army, a decision that would mean that, in the wake of the battle, Marlborough would be able to 'roll up' a number of towns and cities that would ordinarily have been able to resist and tie up his forces, thus slowing down the pace of the campaign.

Numerically, the infantry component of Villeroi's army was similar both in terms of equipment and unit size to its opponent's but, as has been noted, was of far more varying quality – ranging from the veteran units of the French line such as 'Alsace' and 'Picardie' as well as the French and Swiss Guards, through to the replacements which had been rushed to replace the casualties of previous battles as well as the former garrison units. Again, organization was similar to its opponent's, both in unit size and the number of companies, but the primary difference was that the Bourbon forces were trained to fire by rank, which meant that each sub-unit would fire and reload before giving fire again. This meant, naturally, that the volleys were greater in their density, but that there would be pauses between the volleys, which would give the targets time to re-form.

One of the anomalies of French artillery design, this light three-barrelled cannon was presumably designed for an infantry support role, firing multiple charges of canister or grapeshot into the enemy ranks at close range. (Photograph courtesy Iain Stanford)

Understandably enough, Villeroi placed much reliance on his mounted arm, containing as it did a large number of units of the King's household – the Maison du Roi – as well as many veteran regiments of the line, and again, numerically at least, his cavalry had a slight edge over the enemy, but qualitatively the French doctrine for the deployment of dragoons meant that these troops could not really be considered in a comparison of troops that would close 'hand to hand'. Thus, the reality was that in this area Villeroi was at a great disadvantage, which many commentators attribute to the failure to reinforce Taviers successfully when, in reality, they were never part of the true equation. Had the French marshal concentrated these troops in direct support of his infantry lines and deployed the majority of his 'horse' regiments on his open right flank, then things might have developed differently.

Finally, with the addition of Marlborough's siege train to his field artillery, Villeroi found himself literally outgunned, in all senses of the word with perhaps 70 cannon – primarily light pieces – as opposed to almost 120 in the Allied Army. He therefore acted conservatively by deploying a large number of his lighter guns (including perhaps all of the experimental three-barrelled weapons) in support of the positions around Ramillies and Offus, whilst the remainder were used in a counter-role against the Allied infantry and artillery, their effectiveness being possibly enhanced by Marlborough's decision to attack and turn the Bourbon flanks in succession rather than drive straight at the enemy centre.

ORDERS OF BATTLE

THE ALLIED ARMY

General Commanding – His Grace, John Churchill, Duke of
Marlborough (74 battalions, 123 squadrons, 120 guns – 69,000
officers and men)

THE RIGHT WING – CLAUDE-FRÉDÉRIC T'SERCLAES, GRAAF VAN TILLY (54 SQUADRONS – 9,143 OFFICERS AND MEN)

1st Line: Lt. Gen. Lumley (2,492 officers and men)

Hay's Dragoons (British)	2 sqns
Ross's Dragoons (British)	2 sqns
Lumley's Horse (British)	3 sqns
Cadogan's Horse (British)	2 sqns
Schomberg's Horse (British)	2 sqns
Wyndham's Horse (British)	2 sqns
Wood's Horse (British)	2 sqns

Lt. Gen. Dompré (3,100 officers and men)

Gardes Dragonders (Dutch)	5 sqns
Garde du Corps (Dutch)	1 sqn
Opdam's Horse (Dutch)	2 sqns
Fréchapelle's Horse (Hanoverian in Dutch pay)	2 sqns
Chanclos's Horse (Dutch)	2 sqns
Athlone's Horse (Dutch)	2 sqns
Rammingen's Horse (Dutch)	2 sqns
Dompré's Horse (Dutch)	2 sqns

2nd Line: Lt. Gen. Oyen (3,551 officers and men)

Van der Nath Dragoons (Holstein-Gottorp in British pay)	
	4 sqns
Benningsen's Dragoons (Hanoverian in Dutch pay)	3 sqns
Heiden's Horse (Brandenburg in Dutch pay)	2 sqns
Canstein's Horse (Brandenburg in Dutch pay)	2 sqns
Baldwin's Horse (Dutch)	2 sqns
Viettinghoff's Horse (Dutch)	1 sqn
Hünerbein's Horse (Münster in Dutch pay)	2 sqns
Reden's Horse (Hanoverian in Dutch pay)	2 sqns
Hessen-Homburg's Horse (Dutch)	3 sqns

THE CENTRE – GENERAL OF FOOT CHARLES CHURCHILL (47,606 OFFICERS AND MEN)

1st Line:

Lt. Gen., the Earl of Orkney (11,351 officers and men)

Maj. Gen. Withers (4,856 officers and men)

1st Foot Guards (British)	1 bn
Earl of Orkney's Foot/1 (British)	1 bn
Godfrey's Foot (British)	1 bn
Dalrymple's Foot (British)	1 bn
Lalo's Foot (British)	1 bn
Sabine's Foot (British)	1 bn
Webb's Foot (British)	1 bn

Brig. Macartney (4,190 officers and men)

Churchill's Foot (British)	1 bn
Mordaunt's Foot (British)	1 bn
Evans's Foot (British)	1 Bn
Macartney's Foot (British)	1 bn
Stringer's Foot (British)	1 bn
Howe's Foot (British)	1 bn

Brig. Donop (2,305 officers and men)

Garde til Fods (Danish in Dutch pay)	1 bn
Prins Carl/2 (Danish in British pay)	1 bn
Sjaelland/1 (Danish in Dutch pay)	1 bn
Oldenburg (Danish in British pay)	1 bn

Lt. Gen. Spaar (7,228 officers and men)

Maj. Gen. Collier (3,660 officers and men)

Erbprinz von Hesse-Kassel (Brandenburg in British pay)	1 bn
Lattorf (Brandenburg in British pay)	1 bn
Heuckelom (Dutch)	1 bn
Oxenstierna (Swedes in Dutch pay)	1 bn
Capol (Swiss in Dutch pay)	1 bn
Hirzel (Swiss in Dutch pay)	1 bn

Brig. Ziethen (3,568 officers and men)

St Pol (Hanoverian in Dutch pay)	1 bn
Bernsdorff (Hanoverian in Dutch pay)	1 bn
Bruncken (Hanoverian in Dutch pay)	1 bn
Nassau-Usingen (Walloon in Dutch pay)	1 bn
Prinz Ludwig (Hesse-Kassel in Dutch pay)	1 bn
Anhalt-Zerbst (Brandenburg in Dutch pay)	1 bn

Lt. Gen. Dedem (8,474 officers and men)

Maj. Gen. van Soutelande (3,660 officers and men)

Deelen (Dutch)	1 bn
Nassau-Woudenburg (Dutch)	1 bn
Kroonprins (Brandenburg in Dutch pay)	1 bn
Soutelande (Dutch)	1 bn
Tscharner (Swiss in Dutch pay)	1 bn

Maj. Gen. de Vilatte (4,814 officers and men)

Brig. Argyll (Scots Brigade; 2,580 officers and men)

Argyll (Scottish in Dutch pay)	1 bn
Borthwick (Scottish in Dutch pay)	1 bn
Colyear (Scottish in Dutch pay)	1 bn
Murray (Scottish in Dutch pay)	1 bn

Brig. Wassenaer (2,234 officers and men)

Gardes te Voet (Dutch)	3 bns

2nd Line:

Lt. Gen. Ingoldsby (6,235 officers and men)

Brig. Meredith (4,190 officers and men)

Orkney's Foot/2 (British)	1 bn
Ingoldsby's Foot (British)	1 bn
Farrington's Foot (British)	1 bn
Tatton's Foot (British)	1 bn
North's Foot (British)	1 bn

Brig. Schwarztel (2,045 officers and men)

Prins Carl/1 (Danish in British pay)	1 bn
Fynske (Danish in Dutch pay)	1 bn
Württemburg-Oels (Danish in Dutch pay)	1 bn

Lt. Gen. Oxenstierna (7,387 officers and men)

Maj. Gen. Welderen (3,855 officers and men)

Grumbkow (Brandenburg in British pay)	1 bn
Dedem (Dutch)	1 bn
Heyden (Dutch)	1 bn
Els (Dutch)	1 bn
Huffel (Dutch)	1 bn
Jung-Seckendorf (Ansbach-Bayreuth in Dutch pay)	1 bn

Maj. Gen. Bernsdorff (3,532 officers and men)

Rantzow (Hanoverian in Dutch pay)	2 bns
Tecklenburg (Hanoverian in Dutch pay)	1 bn
Veglin (Dutch)	1 bn
Ranck (Dutch)	1 bn
Sturler (Swiss in Dutch pay)	1 bn

Lt. Gen. the Prince of Holstein-Beck (6,931 officers and men

Brig. Keppel (3,185 officers and men)

Aderkas (Holstein-Gottorp in Dutch pay)	1 bn
Barner (Holstein-Gottorp in Dutch pay)	1 bn
Keppel (Dutch)	1 bn
Schwartz (Münster in Dutch pay)	1 bn
Pallandt (Dutch)	1 bn

Maj. Gen. Murray (1,080 officers and men)

Albemarle (Swiss in Dutch pay)	2 bns

Brig. Wermüller (2,666 officers and men)

Salisch (Dutch)	1 bn
Slangenburg (Dutch)	1 bn
Oranje-Friesland (Dutch)	2 bns

THE LEFT WING – GENERAL OF HORSE THE DUKE OF OUWERKERK (12,084 OFFICERS AND MEN)

1st Line: Lt. Gen. Cirksena, Graaf in Ostfriesland (4,523 officers and men)

Maj. Gen. the Prince d'Auvergne (1,408 officers and men)

Cirksena's Horse (Dutch)	2 sqns
Eck's Horse (Dutch)	2 sqns
Pentz's Horse (Hanoverian in Dutch pay)	2 sqns
Rochford's Horse (Dutch)	2 sqns

Brig. Nassau-La Leck (1,476 officers and men)

Nassau-La Leck's Horse (Dutch)	2 sqns
Württemberg's Horse (Dutch)	2 sqns
Cralingen's Horse (Dutch)	2 sqns
Tilly's Horse (Dutch)	2 sqns

Lt. Gen. Dopff (1,639 officers and men)

Blauwe Garde (Dutch)	2 sqns
Carabiniers (Dutch)	4 sqns
Dopff Dragoons (Dutch)	4 sqns

2nd Line: Lt. Gen. Hompesch (3,464 officers and men)

Maj. Gen. St Laurent (1,039 officers and men)

Tengnagel's Horse (Dutch)	2 sqns
Driesbergen's Horse (Dutch)	2 sqns
St Laurent's Horse (Dutch)	2 sqns

Brig. Grovestins (1,476 officers and men)

Grovestins' Horse (Dutch)	2 sqns
Eminga's Horse (Dutch)	2 sqns
Erbach's Horse (Dutch)	2 sqns
Oranje-Friesland's Horse (Dutch)	2 sqns

Brig. Portail (949 officers and men)

Schmettau Dragoons (Ansbach-Bayreuth in Dutch pay)	4 sqns
Baudissin Dragoons (Holstein-Gottorp in British pay)	4 sqns

3rd Line: Lt. Gen. the Prince of Württemberg-Neustadt (4,097 officers and men)

Maj. Gen. Rantzau (1,584 officers and men)

Sjaelland Horse/2 (Danish in Dutch pay)	2 sqns
Holstein's Horse (Danish in British pay)	2 sqns
Württemberg Cuirassiers (Danish in British pay)	2 sqns
Jyske Horse/2 (Danish in British pay)	2 sqns

Brig. Brockdorff (1,606 officers and men)

Jyske Horse/3 (Danish in British pay)	2 sqns
Jyske Horse/4 (Danish in Dutch pay)	2 sqns
Jyske Horse/5 (Danish in Dutch pay)	2 sqns
Liv regiment til Hest (Danish in Dutch pay)	2 sqns

Brig. Bonnart (907 officers and men)

Württemberg-Oels Dragoons (Danish in Dutch pay)	5 sqns

ARTILLERY

The exact composition of Marlborough's artillery train at Ramillies remains unclear but, from what we do know of the English Field Train under Colonel Holcroft Blood and the accepted ratios of guns to men, a reasonable assumption would be as follows:

Dutch Field Train:	6 x 12-pdr, 10 x 6–8-pdr, 32 x 3-pdr
English Field Train:	6 x 12-pdr, 10 x 6–8-pdr, 16 x 3-pdr, 4 x howitzer
Dutch Siege Train:	20 x 24-pdr, 4 x howitzer, 12 x mortar

THE ARMY OF THE TWO CROWNS

General Commanding – His Grace, François de Neufville, Duc de Villeroi (70 battalions, 132 squadrons, 70 guns – 62,000 officers and men)

THE RIGHT WING – MAXIMILIAN II EMANUEL VON WITTELSBACH, ELECTORAL PRINCE OF BAVARIA

Franquenée Garrison (535 officers and men)	
Rohan-Chabot Dragoons (French)	3 sqns
Pignatelli Dragoons (Walloon in Spanish service)	1 sqn
Taviers Garrison (640 officers and men)	
Greder/3 (Swiss in French service)	1 bn

1st Line: (5,993 officers and men)

Lt. Gen. de Guiscard (3,315 officers and men)

Brig. Montesson (Maison du Roi)	
Maison Rouge (1,060 officers and men)	
Chevauxlégers de la Garde (French)	1 sqn
Gendarmerie de la Garde (French)	1 sqn
1ère Compagnie de Mousquetaires (French)	1 sqn
2e Companie de Mousquetaires (French)	1 sqn
Grenadiers à Cheval de la Garde (French)	1 sqn
Garde du Corps (1,720 officers and men)	
1ère Compagnie des Gardes du Corps (French)	2 sqns
2e Compagnie des Gardes du Corps (French)	2 sqns
3e Compagnie des Gardes du Corps (French)	2 sqns
4e Compagnie des Gardes du Corps (French)	2 sqns
Brig. Nill (535 officers and men)	
Tarente Horse (French)	2 sqns
Courcillion Horse (French)	2 sqns

Lt. Gen. Chimay (2,678 officers and men)

Brig. Desmarets (1,202 officers and men)	
Desmarets Horse (French)	2 sqns
du Maine Horse (French)	3 sqns
Gacé Horse (French)	2 sqns
Roye Horse (French)	2 sqns
Brig. Fraula (1,476 officers and men)	
Fresin Horse (Spanish)	2 sqns
Gaetano Horse (Spanish – Tercio)	2 sqns
Fraula Horse (Italian – Tercio)	2 sqns
Costa Horse (German in Spanish service)	2 sqns
Heyder Horse (Spanish – Tercio)	2 sqns

Chimay's brigades with the Rohan-Chabot and Pignatelli dragoons from Marsin

2nd Line: (4,166 officers and men)

Lt. Gen. Gassion (2,189 officers and men)

Verseilles Hussars (400 men; French)	3 sqns
Brig. Mimur (961 officers and men)	
Toulouse Horse (French)	3 sqns
Royal-Étranger Horse (French)	3 sqns
Brig. Apelterre (828 officers and men)	
Egmont Horse (Spanish)	2 sqns
Aubusson Horse (French)	2 sqns

Bellefonds Horse (French)	2 sqns

Lt. Gen. Roussy (1,977 officers and men)

Brig. Bar (561 officers and men)	
Toulongeon Horse (Burgundian – Tercio)	2 sqns
Bar Horse (French)	2 sqns
Brig. Nugent (561 officers and men)	
Lacotoire Horse (Walloon – Tercio)	2 sqns
Nugent Horse (Irish in French service)	2 sqns
Brig. Mortani (855 officers and men)	
Beaussart Horse (Walloon – Tercio)	2 sqns
Royal Allemand Horse (German in French service)	3 sqns

3rd Line: Lt. Gen. the Chevalier de Rohan-Chabot (1,970 officers and men)

Brig. Nothafft von Weißenstein (1,165 officers and men)	
Leib Dragoons (Cologne)	2 sqns
Acquaviva Dragoons (Spanish)	3 sqns
Dragons du Roi (French)	3 sqns

Brig. Ferrare (805 officers and men)

Aubigné Dragoons (French)	3 sqns
Ferrare Dragoons (Spanish)	3 sqns

Supports: Lt. Gen. Biron (5,585 officers and men)

Maj. Gen. La Mothe (2,385 officers and men)	
Brig. Wolfskehl (1,350 officers and men)	
Wolfskehl (Cologne)	1 bn
Kurprinz (Bavaria)	2 bns
Brig. Nonan (1,035 officers and men)	
Provence (French)	1 bn
Bassigny/2 (French)	1 bn
Maj. Gen. Sézanne (3,200 officers and men)	
Brig. Villars (1,920 officers and men)	
Villars (Swiss in French service)	3 bns
Brig. Greder (1,280 officers and men)	
Greder/1 and 2 (Swiss in French service)	2 bns

RAMILLIES SECTOR (11,147 OFFICERS AND MEN)

Lt. Gen. d'Artagnan (6,241 officers and men)

Maj. Gen. Marchese di Maffei (2,480 officers and men)

Gardes de Cologne (Cologne)	2 bns
Gardes de Bavière (Bavaria)	3 bns
Brig. Seluc (2,208 officers and men)	
Picardie (French)	3 bns
Clare (Irish in French service)	1 bn
Brig. Albergotti (1,553 officers and men)	
Gondrin (French)	2 bns
Royal Italien (Italian in French service)	1 bn

Lt. Gen. Lede (4,406 officers and men)

Brig. Steckenberg (2,208 officers and men)	
Alsace (French)	4 bns
Brig. P. Grimaldi (1,035 officers and men)	
Nice (French)	1 bn
St Segond (French)	1 bn
Brig. Nassau (1,163 officers and men)	

Nassau (Spanish)	1 bn
Holstein (Spanish)	1 bn

OFFUS SECTOR:(13,368 OFFICERS AND MEN)

Lt. Gen. Surville (8,000 officers and men)

Brig. Montpesat (6,080 officers and men)

Gardes Françaises (3,680 men) (French)	6 bns
Gardes Suisses (1,600 men) (Swiss in French service)	3 bns

Brig. Besenval (1,920 officers and men)

Castellas (Swiss in French service)	3 bns

Lt. Gen. de Villeroi (3,106 officers and men)

Brig. La Marck (1,553 officers and men)

La Marck (French)	2 bns
Montroux (French)	1 bn

Brig. Isenghien (1,553 officers and men)

St Sulpice (French)	2 bns
Isenghien (French)	1 bn

Lt. Gen. P. Grimaldi (2,262 officers and men)

Brig. St Pierre (1,099 officers and men)

Fisileros de Flandres (Spanish–Walloon)	1 bn
St Vallier (French)	1 bn

Brig. Lede (1,163 officers and men)

Lede (Spanish)	1 bn
Bournonville (Spanish)	1 bn

AUTRE-ÉGLISE SECTOR: (9,990 OFFICERS AND MEN)

Lt. Gen. d'Antin (5,584 officers and men)

Brig. Pfeiffer (3,840 officers and men)

Hessy (Swiss in French service)	3 bns
Pfeiffer (Swiss in French service)	3 bns

Brig. A Grimaldi (1,744 officers and men)

Grimberghes (Spanish)	1 bn
de Laernes (Spanish)	1 bn
Grimaldi (Spanish)	1 bn

Lt. Gen. Birkenfeld (4,406 officers and men)

Brig. Zuniga (2,198 officers and men)

Sparre (French)	2 bns
Courrières (Spanish)	1 bn
Zuniga (Spanish)	1 bn

Brig. Barial (2,208 officers and men)

Le Roi (French)	4 bns

BETWEEN RAMILLIES AND OFFUS: LT. GEN. HORN (2,848 OFFICERS AND MEN)

Brig. Beringhen (693 officers and men)

Beringhen Horse (French)	3 sqns
Cano Horse (Spanish)	2 sqns

Brig. Costa (1,485 officers and men)

Dobbelstein Horse (Cologne)	2 sqns
Wolframsdorff Horse (Bavaria)	3 sqns
Costa Horse (Bavaria)	3 sqns
Prinz Philipp Carabiniers (Bavaria)	3 sqns

Brig. Chassonville (670 officers and men)

Chassonville Dragoons (Cologne)	2 sqns
Bretagne Dragoons (French)	3 sqns

BETWEEN OFFUS AND AUTRE-ÉGLISE: LT. GEN. EGMONT (4,169 OFFICERS AND MEN)

Brig. Rosen (829 officers and men)

Royal Cravattes (French)	3 sqns
Rosen Horse (French)	2 sqns

Brig. Weickel (1,080 officers and men)

Leibregiment zu Pferd (Cologne)	2 sqns
Weickel Cuirassiers (Bavaria)	3 sqns
Arco (Bavaria)	3 sqns

Brig. Santini (1,050 officers and men)

Guardia Wallonia (Spain–Walloon)	3 sqns
Leibregiment zu Pferd (Cologne)	1 sqn
Leibregiment zu Pferd (Bavaria)	3 sqns

Brig. d'Escorial (1,210 officers and men)

Pasteur Dragoons (Spain)	3 sqns
Rysbourg Dragoons (Spain)	3 sqns
Maître-General de Camp Dragoons (French)	3 sqns

ARTILLERY

Royal Artillery	1 bn, 500 officers and men
Bombardiers	1 bn, 500 officers and men
Spanish, Bavarian and Cologne	500 officers and men
Total	2 bns, 1,500 officers and men

As with the Allied Army, the exact details of the artillery deployed by the Bourbon forces vary over a number of differing accounts but, given standard French practice, we can reasonably estimate the number and type of cannon as follows:

12 x 16–24-pdr, 20 x 6–12-pdr, 38 x 4-pdr

Given the above, the French train would have consisted of between 40 and 44 artillery pieces, with the remainder comprising the Spanish train.

It should be noted, however, that the above poundages are given using French measurements and are slightly heavier than their English counterparts. Therefore, the triple-barrelled cannon captured in Ramillies village would have been classed as light guns in the French army, and possibly as medium by their captors; under English measurements, the example on display at the Royal Artillery Museum in London, is classified as a 5.5-pdr.

OPPOSING PLANS

THE ALLIED ARMY

Marlborough began the Ramillies campaign with but one simple aim in mind: irrespective of how large the Bourbon field army would prove to be, and irrespective of its location, he would seek it out and destroy it. Confident of success, he therefore insisted that the army's siege train march with the main body in order to exploit any victory rather than having to be called forward once the army encountered resistance. As such, having the option of using the train as heavy field pieces would give Marlborough an almost insurmountable advantage over Villeroi. It was therefore to his great delight that Cadogan's advance party reported encountering the enemy picquets, and from that moment he began to apply himself to adopting a conventional deployment that would allow him to react quickly to any changes in the battle.

Unable to study the enemy positions because of the early morning mist, Marlborough elected to deploy in a seemingly conventional manner, with an infantry centre flanked by two cavalry wings, the former being commanded by his younger brother – Charles Churchill – and the latter being commanded by Ouwerkerk and Tilly. The reason for the qualification to the Allied deployment was that Marlborough saw that the key to the battle would not be the various

This 19th-century French engraving shows the whole theatre of operations for May 1706. With Ramillies in the lower centre, the Allies' advance is from Orp le Grand in the upper right-hand side of the map, whilst the Bourbon forces came south from Jodoigne in the upper centre of the map. (Author's collection)

The military situation, May 1706

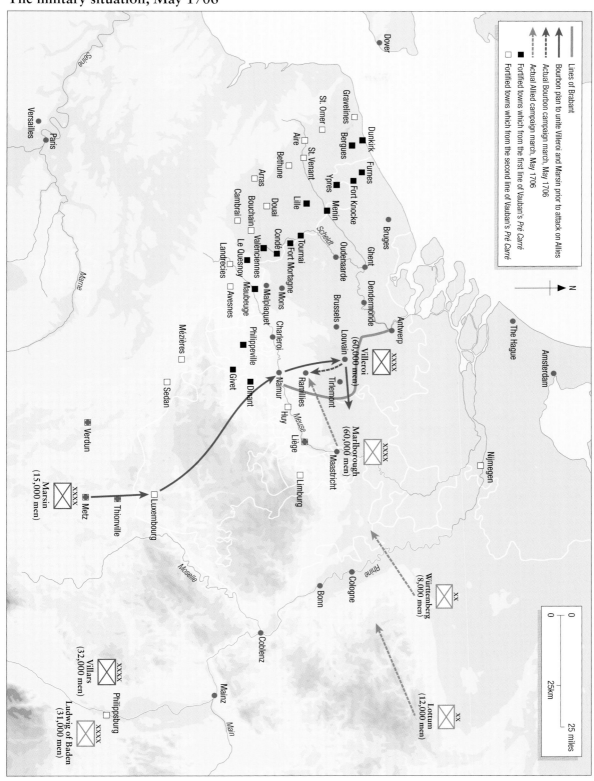

villages which formed bastions along the Bourbon front line, but rather the open terrain to the south of Ramillies, which would, once secured, grant egress to the enemy's rear and line of retreat. He therefore decided to detach a brigade of foot to sweep down the valley of the Mehaigne to Taviers with orders to clear out any enemy troops, whilst simultaneously massing his British brigades on the extreme right of the infantry line placing them in a position to attack the village of Autre-Église, the anchor point of the Bourbon left flank. The reasons for this were twofold: firstly, by deploying his own countrymen in such a fashion, he hoped to persuade Villeroi that he was more concerned about making progress on his right flank – after all this was the shortest route onto the enemy's assumed line of retreat – and secondly that if sufficient progress were to be made, then the Earl of Orkney, commanding the British brigades, was the officer most likely to capitalize successfully on this.

Once it was clear that Villeroi had taken the 'bait' and reinforced his left by drawing troops from elsewhere along his battle line and, once the flanking brigade had been confirmed in possession of Taviers, Marlborough then intended to launch simultaneous attacks against the Bourbon right wing, with his own left-wing cavalry under Ouwerkerk. He also planned to attack the village of Ramillies, at the extreme end of the Bourbon centre with a dedicated force of infantry whose job would be to attack the village and draw as many enemy troops into the street fighting which would prevent those nearest the cavalry mêlée from supporting the Bourbon horsemen.

With a slightly shorter frontage than that of the enemy, the remainder of the army was deployed in such a way as to enable Marlborough to shift units quickly as changes in the battle might dictate, thereby maintaining pressure on the enemy and increasing the likelihood of his achieving the decisive victory that he sought in order to break the stalemate enforced by the sedentary nature of the conflict in the Low Countries.

This stylized print by the Victorian artist, Richard Caton-Woodville, shows a white-coated Régiment de Clare in action against an unknown British infantry regiment. In reality, Clare was engaged against the Dutch Scots Brigade within the centre of Ramillies village. (Author's collection)

THE ARMY OF THE TWO CROWNS

Even at this remove from the Court at Versailles, King Louis's wishes carried great force, expressed in admonitions about the reliability of the allied contingents present with the army – that they were not to be deployed in complete formations of their own nationality – and indeed the King's letter of 6 May, in which he wrote of his desire for a peaceful settlement but only one that was dictated by France: 'Je ne vois rien qui puisse mieux les déterminer à venir à un accommodement qui est devenu nécessaire, que de leur fair voir que j'ai des forces suffisantes pour les attaquer partout'. In short, the Allies must be defeated in the field and Villeroi took this as being an admonition that, just as on the Rhine or in Spain and Northern Italy, the Bourbon forces should take the offensive, the series of victories envisaged by the 'Sun King' would serve to force the enemy to the negotiating table.

With this – single – error of judgement, Villeroi possibly lost his campaign before his troops marched into battle for, as a lesser warrior than either Villars in Germany, Vendôme in Italy or Berwick in Spain, all he would have to do was not lose against Marlborough in order to achieve the royal objectives. Instead, and in order to achieve numerical parity with his opponent, he opted to increase the size of his field army by stripping the garrisons from a number of towns and cities and adding the units to his main body. Thus, with the new drafts required by the defeats of the previous two years, he would be taking the field with an army that was, to a degree, brittle. There were a number of veteran corps in the army's ranks as well as the elite units of the Gardes and Maison du Roi, but taken as a whole, it was probably not an army designed for offensive action.

Again, Caton-Woodville fuses disparate elements of the battle to construct a rousing image. Here Marlborough forms the British cavalry prior to launching an attack. In reality the British cavalry was engaged on the right flank, whilst Marlborough's command post was in the centre of the battlefield. (Author's collection)

In addition to the above, Villeroi was to be reinforced by Marsin who had concluded his joint operations with Villars and, having sent a force of 20 squadrons of cavalry forward under the Prince de Chimay to join his colleague, was himself now between Metz and Namur heading northwards at best possible speed.

That said, Villeroi's deployment was a reasonable one. A number of modern authors have shown the Bourbon battle lines as stretching in a curved half-moon from Autre-Église in the north, southwards through Ramillies to Taviers, and have used this to decry his deployment and therefore his plan of battle. Yet it should be made clear that the line ended at Ramillies, with the right-wing cavalry being refused and slightly to the rear of the village, that they would advance into the 'gap' only in response to Ouwerkerk's advance, and that Taviers and Franquenée were merely outposts designed to slow the enemy advance along the valley of the Mehaigne.

With Guiscard's horsemen covering the open right flank, the French marshal fortified the three villages of Ramillies, Offus and Autre-Église and used them as strongpoints to anchor the army behind the line of the Petite Gheete and its various tributaries. He planned to use the adverse terrain to break up the enemy attacks and then beat them on the counter with infantry attacks supported by cavalry brigades deployed slightly to the rear of the main body.

It was a reasonable, albeit in the end risky, deployment as doing by so he naturally – and rather dangerously – surrendered the initiative to his opponent, and yet one must give Villeroi the benefit of the doubt for had La Motte been more expeditious in the execution of his orders and occupied Taviers with his full battalion, or indeed had Villeroi ensured that the whole of the Greder regiment had been sent there, then it would most likely have thrown out Marlborough's fine sense of timing, and he would almost certainly have had to delay or even postpone his own main attacks and reconsider his whole tactical plan as the fighting continued.

THE BATTLE

APPROACH TO CONTACT

During the early hours of 23 May – Whitsunday – 1706, a large body of men rode out of the Allied camp around the village of Corswarem. Commanded by Marlborough's Quartermaster General, William Cadogan, and comprising the regimental quartermasters escorted by 600 men of the 'day guard', their task was routine – to scout ahead of the army and reconnoitre a suitable campsite for the end of the day's march, one which would take the Duke's forces to within striking distance of the Franco-Spanish forces under Villeroi, who were known to be holding a position on the line of the Dyle around the town of Jodoignes.

Although Cadogan's scout was in theory an easy one – westwards by road towards Jandrenouille and the plateau to which the village gave its name and then following the line of the Petite Gheete towards Ramillies, and thence west onto the plateau of Mont St André – the practicalities of the route were far from easy, the torrential rain of the preceding days having turned the terrain into a quagmire which forced the column to remain on the roads, and then, as the sun rose, a heavy fog began to settle, obscuring visibility in all directions.

Onwards the small column pressed until about 8.00am when they reached the hamlet of Merdorp on the plateau of Jandrenouille. After a short pause to allow the tail end of the formation to catch up, the troopers set off again towards the south-west and as they ascended to the higher ground, it was a case of the utmost good luck that they were to make out the shadowy outline of horsemen to their front, men who could belong only to the enemy army. A brief but ineffective exchange of fire saw the shadows disperse, but to Cadogan the situation was clear – Villeroi had not remained on the Dyle and was evidently a lot closer to the Allied Army than anyone had anticipated.

The starting point – the view southwards from the Plateau of Jandrenouille following Marlborough's line of advance, before the army began its deployment for battle around Foulx. (Copyright and courtesy of Seán Ó'Brógáin)

The march to battle

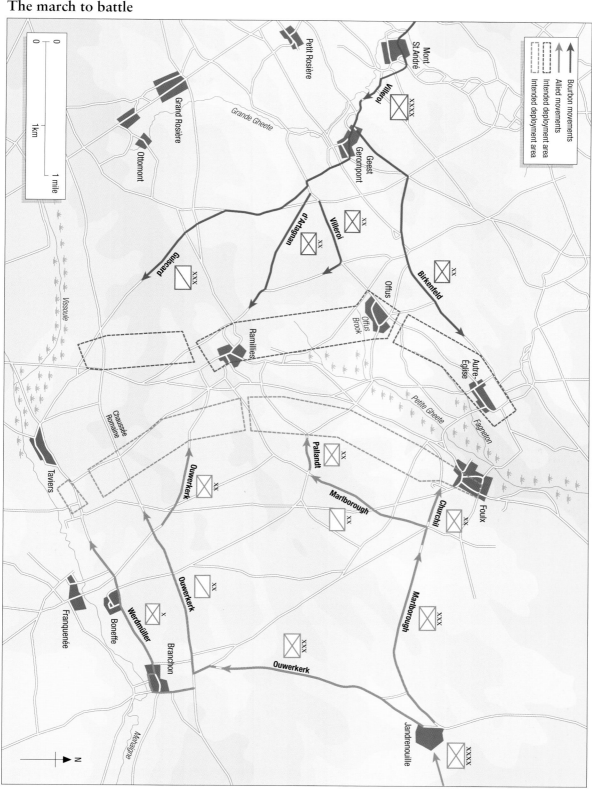

The valley of the Mehaigne, as seen from Taviers churchyard. At the time of the battle much of this ground would have been waterlogged and heavy going for both armies. (Copyright and courtesy of Seán Ó'Brógáin)

Reining in, and deciding that little would be served if he were to blunder into overwhelming numbers of the enemy, Cadogan immediately sent an aide galloping back to Marlborough's headquarters to inform the Duke of this latest intelligence and then took station in anticipation that the fog would rise; with the improved visibility he would be able to provide his commanding officer with a more accurate appraisal of the situation.

The courier found Marlborough with the leading elements of the army which had halted in order that the rearward columns could close up with the main body, and, as soon as he had digested the intelligence report, he gave orders that the closest cavalry formations should be rushed forward to Cadogan's position. Then, flanked by a number of senior officers and his headquarters staff, the Duke put spurs to horse to join the Quartermaster General and see the situation for himself.

Marlborough's party joined Cadogan's force a little before 10.00am, and after a hurried conference the Irishman began to outline to his commander the enemy positions on the Mont St André on the opposite side of the valley of the Petite Gheete. Unsure of the enemy's numbers or intentions, Marlborough now decided to force the issue by sending a strong cavalry force forward to sweep them from the eminence. It was now that the fog finally began to clear and, as it did so, the Allied commander was granted the view of not just a detachment of Villeroi's force but also of the whole Army of the Two Crowns, deploying for battle on the terrain that he himself had intended to occupy that evening.

It is unclear how much of a shock the enemy presence was to Marlborough, but any such surprise was soon subordinated by the activities of a professional soldier engaged in his *métier*. Couriers were soon beating their way back along the line of march to hurry the troops forward and a messenger was also dispatched to the Duke of Württemberg-Neustadt, in command of the Danish contingent, who still had to effect a junction with the main body of the army, requesting him to make the best possible time. In any event, it had been Marlborough's intention to force a battle wherever the enemy should be found and, with the initial preparations to consolidate the army now under way, he began to outline his intentions to his principal subordinates. Many of these officers had implicit trust in their commander and listened attentively as he outlined his plans, but inevitably there was a voice of dissent, that of Sicco van Goslinga, one of the Dutch 'field deputies' attached to the army as a political liaison between the Dutch Government and the army. As far as the Dutchman could see, 'The enemy's left could not be attacked with a prospect of success; for the hedges, ditches and marshes were a complete barrier to both sides; that therefore the whole of our cavalry should be massed on our left, even if they had to be three or four lines deep there.'

In a similar vein, Goslinga continued to opine that the Allied Army was now dangerously exposed, with its commander at the tip of the spearhead and the main body strung out on a series of roads of dubious quality and that all it would take would be an aggressive move from Villeroi towards the plateau of Jandrenouille to scatter the marching columns and defeat the Allies in detail. Marlborough listened politely as such pessimistic advice was delivered and then promptly chose to ignore it; after all if – as Goslinga had eloquently stated – the terrain was disadvantageous to both armies, then Villeroi would himself surely be courting disaster if he were now to come off the ridgeline and attempt to force a passage eastwards. In effect, by adopting the position that he had, the French commander had committed himself to a defensive engagement; the only question which remained was whether it would be based on the position that he now held, or one intended to cover a retreat to the Dyle.

Across the valley of the Gheete, Villeroi was also reaching a decision about the impending engagement. Having received the reports from the picquets that had encountered Cadogan on the plateau of Jandrenouille, he could not fail to realize that the opening stages of the battle that he had so openly sought were unfolding before his very eyes and yet his co-commander Maximilian, Elector of Bavaria, was absent from the army, having spent the previous evening attending a Pentecost celebration in Brussels. Deciding to fight a defensive battle, Villeroi chose to anchor his left flank upon the hamlets of Offus and Autre-Église on the Plateau de Mont St André in the north and his centre upon the village of Ramillies in the valley of the Petite Gheete, with his right flank resting on the rising ground between Ramillies and the river Mehaigne to the south. Having made his dispositions and as the troops moved forward into position, a courier was sent to Brussels to hasten the Elector to the battlefield.

Although modern drainage has altered its profile, this close-up of the Fagneton stream gives a good impression of the obstacle it posed to the infantry under Orkney's command. (Copyright and courtesy of Seán Ó'Brógáin)

THE GROUND

Despite later critiques, the position was relatively strong, and easily given over to defence – the settlements were studded with solidly built farmhouses, typical of the region, such as the Haute Cense and Basse Cense around Ramillies, which could easily be fortified as redoubts, as would be their near neighbours Hougoumont and La Haye Sainte almost a century later. In the north, the approaches to Autre-Église were shielded by no less than four waterways – the Communes, Fagneton, Frambais and the Petite Gheete, each of which, whilst normally only a stream a yard or two across, combined with the recent heavy rainfall to provide the hamlet with a watery shield, which attacking troops would find difficult indeed, if not impossible, to pentrate. To its front, Offus was similarly protected by the Petite Gheete, whilst its northern and southern approaches were screened by the Fagneton and the Offus brook respectively. At Ramillies itself, the Petite Gheete swung behind the village and forked, close to the hedged fields, and, whilst this would hamper an immediate reinforcement in the event of the village

This 19th-century plan of the battle of Ramillies clearly shows how misconceptions regarding the armies' deployments have become part of the literary canon. Here both Taviers and Franquenée are shown as being to the south-west of the village of Ramillies rather than to the south-east as they actually are. (Author's collection)

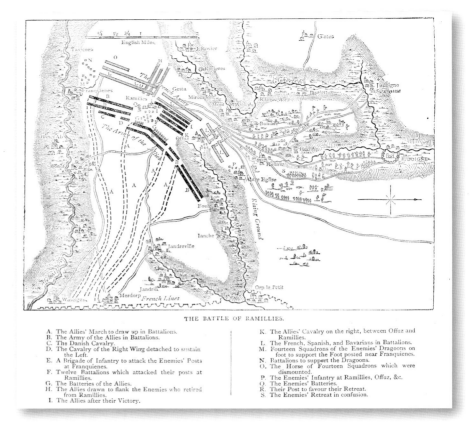

THE BATTLE OF RAMILLIES.

A. The Allies' March to draw up in Battalions.
B. The Army of the Allies in Battalions.
C. The Danish Cavalry.
D. The Cavalry of the Right Wing detached to sustain the Left.
E. A Brigade of Infantry to attack the Enemies' Posts at Franquienes.
F. Twelve Battalions which attacked their posts at Ramillies.
G. The Batteries of the Allies.
H. The Allies drawn to flank the Enemies who retired from Ramillies.
I. The Allies after their Victory.

K. The Allies' Cavalry on the right, between Offuz and Ramillies.
L. The French, Spanish, and Bavarians in Battalions.
M. Fourteen Squadrons of the Enemies' Dragoons on foot to support the Foot posted near Franquienes.
N. Battalions to support the Dragoons.
O. The Horse of Fourteen Squadrons which were dismounted.
P. The Enemies' Infantry at Ramillies, Offuz, &c.
Q. The Enemies' Batteries.
R. Their Post to favour their Retreat.
S. The Enemies' Retreat in confusion.

needing to be urgently reinforced, it would also serve to bolster the defences should the garrison be surrounded, similar to Clérambault's force at Blindheim two years previously.

To the south of Ramillies and in seeming contradiction to most published maps, the terrain – whilst less undulating – rises sharply before descending slightly into the valley of the Mehaigne and its tributaries. It is an area, which, far from being the 'perfect cavalry terrain' as described by a number of modern authors, nonetheless remains the only area of the battlefield bereft of water features, and it was inevitable that this would be where each commander would deploy the majority of his mounted troops.

THE FRENCH DEPLOY

The extreme left flank was commanded by Christian II von Wittelsbach, Graf von Birkenfeld-Zweibrücken, and consisted of a mixed Franco-Spanish brigade of four battalions, which occupied Autre-Église supported by the four-battalion Régiment du Roi, the colonel of which was King Louis XIV himself. To Birkenfeld's right and extending the line through to Offus, stood two brigades of foot under the command of the Marquis d'Antin (six battalions of Swiss under Pfeiffer and three Spanish under Antonio Ceva di Grimaldi) with four brigades of mounted troops (three of horse and one of dragoons) totalling 29 squadrons, in support, these last being eminently placed to sweep into the flank of any enemy attack on either hamlet.

Offus, the junction between the left flank and the centre, was held by two French brigades, those of Isenghien and La Marck, with the three-battalion French regiment of Castellas to their rear in direct support; to their right and continuing the line southwards towards Ramillies stood the nine battalions of the combined Gardes Françaises and Gardes Suisses under the Marquis de Montpesat. Two small – predominantly Spanish – brigades, those of St Pierre and Lede were posted to the rear of Montpesat's formation in support.

The key to the French line was inevitably based upon Ramillies, a village of fewer than 200 inhabitants, the defence of which was placed under the overall command of Pierre, Comte d'Artagnan. To the north of the village stood the units of the Bourbon 'right centre' which consisted of the four battalions of the French 'Alsace' regiment, under Steckenberg *vice* its colonel, Birkenfeld, who commanded at Autre-Église, the formation being supported by the small brigades of the Marcello Ceva di Grimaldi and Francisco de Nassau, each comprising two battalions of French and Spanish troops respectively. Adjacent to 'Alsace' stood two brigades under the command of Charles O'Brien, Viscount Clare. The first brigade, consisting of Clare's own regiment and that of 'Picardie' – the senior 'line' formation of the French infantry – was under the direct command of the Comte Seluc, and extended the army's front into the northern part of Ramillies. To Seluc's rear stood Clare's second brigade consisting of three French battalions under Albergotti. The southern part of the village was commanded by the Marchese di Maffei, an Italian officer in Bavarian service, who commanded the Leibregimente zu Fuß of the Bavarian Elector and his brother, the exiled Archbishop of Cologne.

In support of his infantry, d'Artagnan deployed three groups of cavalry disposing a total of 29 squadrons. In the front line were the brigades of

This close-up of the fortified gateway of the Cense de la Tour in Offus shows exactly what a tough proposition these buildings would pose to attackers, exactly as Hougoumont and La Haye Sainte would pose to the French at Waterloo, a century later. (Copyright and courtesy of Seán Ó'Brógáin)

Contemporary print showing Marlborough and his headquarters staff as the battle rages around them. Ramillies church can be clearly made out in the centre of the image, with Offus on a high ridge to the right, looming over Autre-Église. The cavalry mêlée continues to the left of the image. (Courtesy and copyright of la Bibliothèque Nationale de France)

View looking northwards from the Tomb of Ottomond across the deployment area of the Bourbon right flank. The steeple of Ramillies church can be seen towards the centre-left of the image. (Copyright and courtesy of Seán Ó'Brógáin)

La Ferme de la Château, between Taviers and Franquenée, one of the potential 'choke points' that Marlborough feared would hinder the advance of his left wing, hence his decision to send Werdmüller to sweep the Mehaigne Valley clear of enemy troops. (Copyright and courtesy of Seán Ó'Brógáin)

Beringhen and Costa commanding Franco-Spanish and Bavarian-Cologne horse regiments respectively, whilst the formation's third line was formed from Cologne's Chassonville dragoons paired with the French Bretagne regiment.

Given the relatively open terrain – and in anticipation that his opponent would do the same – Villeroi deployed the bulk of his cavalry to cover the army's 'open' right flank, entrusting the command of this vital sector to Lt. Gen. the Marquis de Guiscard.

Suitably enough, the position of honour at the head of the Bourbon left flank was given over to the proud horsemen of the Maison du Roi, the French king's household troops, who were flanked by the regiments of 'Tarente' and 'Courcillion'. Directly behind, the Prince de Chimay led a further two brigades of horse – one French and one Spanish – bringing the first line up to a total strength of 36 squadrons.

Supporting Guiscard, the second line of cavalry was commanded by the Comte de Gassion directly commanding five regiments of Franco-Spanish horse, attached to which were the Verseilles Hussars, a colourful unit originally formed in 1692 but whose members had – until recently – been distributed amongst several regiments of horse until it was decided that their scouting capabilities would be of significant use in the field. To the rear of Gassion's command stood a further three brigades of Franco-Spanish horse led by the Comte de Roussy, comprising a further six regiments. All told, a further 28 squadrons formed up under Gassion's command.

The definition of the third and final line of mounted troops on the Bourbon right flank is one that causes significant confusion in many narratives of the battle. Consisting of three regiments of French, three of Spanish and one of Cologne dragoons, conventional doctrine stated that

these troops would not be deployed against enemy cavalry but rather to hold terrain features and generally support the front-line troops. As such, their commander the Chevalier de Rohan-Chabot was obliged to deploy two of his regiments to hold the forward position around the farm of Franquenée, whilst the remaining units – some 14 squadrons – were held as an ultimate flank reserve, for deployment as circumstances dictated.

FIRST BLOOD

With the final approach of his marching columns, and their gradual movement into line of battle, Marlborough decided to secure his left flank by detaching a brigade of troops to clear any enemy forces from the settlements in the Mehaigne Valley and thus facilitate the eventual deployment of his left-wing cavalry. As a signal honour to his Dutch allies, he gave the task to Hans Felix Werdmüller, colonel of the Albemarle regiment of foot. An experienced officer, the Swiss had begun his career as an officer in a French cavalry regiment in 1676, transferring into the Gardes Suisses three years later. In 1688 he was obliged to quit French service when the cantonal government of Zurich enacted a law which prevented its citizens from serving Louis XIV. Five years later he entered Dutch service as a major in a Swiss subsidy regiment, eventually being promoted to Colonel-Commandant of the Albemarle regiment, later serving at the sieges of Bonn and Trarbach and the battles of Blenheim and the Schellenberg.

To accomplish the task, Werdmüller was given three regiments of foot: the two-battalion 'Oranje Friesland' and the single-battalion 'Salisch' and 'Slangenberg' regiments, to which were added two light guns for direct support. Marching south from Jandrenouille to the Mehaigne, Werdmüller first secured Branchon and then Boneffe, dominated by the remains of its 13th-century abbey. However, as the column continued farther along the valley, the advance was brought to an abrupt halt by an eruption of musketry from the walls and hedges that lined the farmhouse at Franquenée, occupied by dragoons of the 'Pignatelli' and 'Rohan-Chabot' regiments who had been placed there to give advance warning of any Allied attempt to force the Mehaigne. Deploying off the road, the Dutch infantry began to advance towards the enemy position, pausing on the word of command to fire rippling volleys in the direction of the concealed enemy. The firefight was short and one sided as the Bourbons were greatly outnumbered with nothing that could answer Werdmüller's artillery detachment, and as riders were dispatched to the Comte de Guiscard, commanding the right-flank cavalry, the Bourbon troops withdrew towards Taviers. This was the next settlement on the enemy's line of march and one that – according to Villeroi's plan of battle – should already be held in sufficient numbers to blunt the Allies' advance.

Taviers, standing above the confluence of the Mehaigne and the Vissoule stream, was the key to the Bourbon right flank. Situated on the northern slopes of the river valley, it consisted of a dozen or so buildings congregated around the parish church. With this higher area surrounded by hedged fields, in contrast to the river valley that was a sodden morass, it was a natural bottleneck that could choke Marlborough's flanking manoeuvre before it could even develop. But as the dragoons withdrew from their advanced position and instead of the three veteran battalions that Villeroi had earmarked for the defence of the village – the other two battalions remained in position behind Ramillies – they found but one company, not more than 200 men, of the

View looking directly eastwards from the Tomb of Ottomond towards Taviers and the Allied approach routes. The Bourbon right flank would have been deployed to the left of the image. (Copyright and courtesy of Seán Ó'Brógáin)

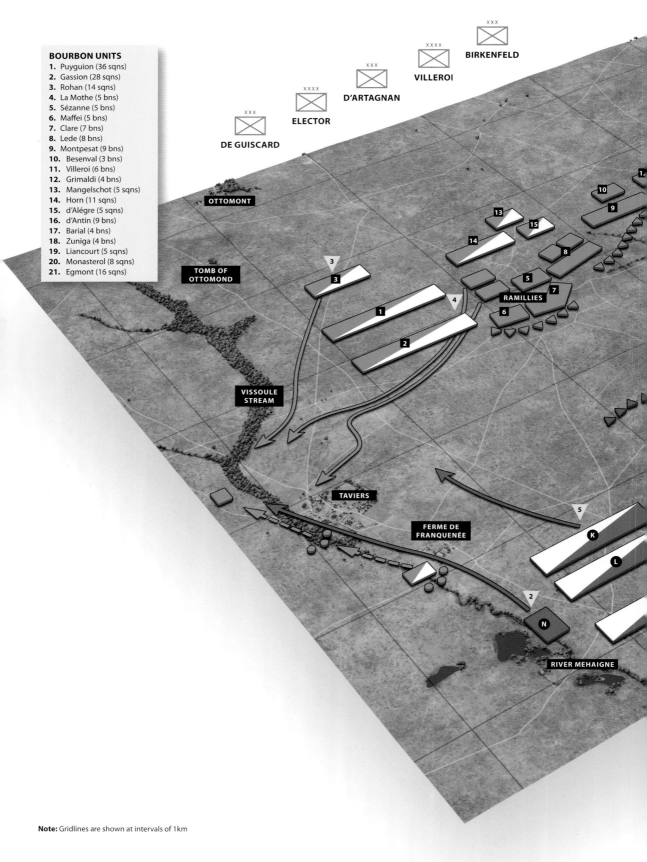

BOURBON UNITS

1. Puyguion (36 sqns)
2. Gassion (28 sqns)
3. Rohan (14 sqns)
4. La Mothe (5 bns)
5. Sézanne (5 bns)
6. Maffei (5 bns)
7. Clare (7 bns)
8. Lede (8 bns)
9. Montpesat (9 bns)
10. Besenval (3 bns)
11. Villeroi (6 bns)
12. Grimaldi (4 bns)
13. Mangelschot (5 sqns)
14. Horn (11 sqns)
15. d'Alégre (5 sqns)
16. d'Antin (9 bns)
17. Barial (4 bns)
18. Zuniga (4 bns)
19. Liancourt (5 sqns)
20. Monasterol (8 sqns)
21. Egmont (16 sqns)

DE GUISCARD

ELECTOR

D'ARTAGNAN

VILLEROI

BIRKENFELD

OTTOMONT

TOMB OF
OTTOMOND

RAMILLIES

VISSOULE
STREAM

TAVIERS

FERME DE
FRANQUENÉE

RIVER MEHAIGNE

Note: Gridlines are shown at intervals of 1km

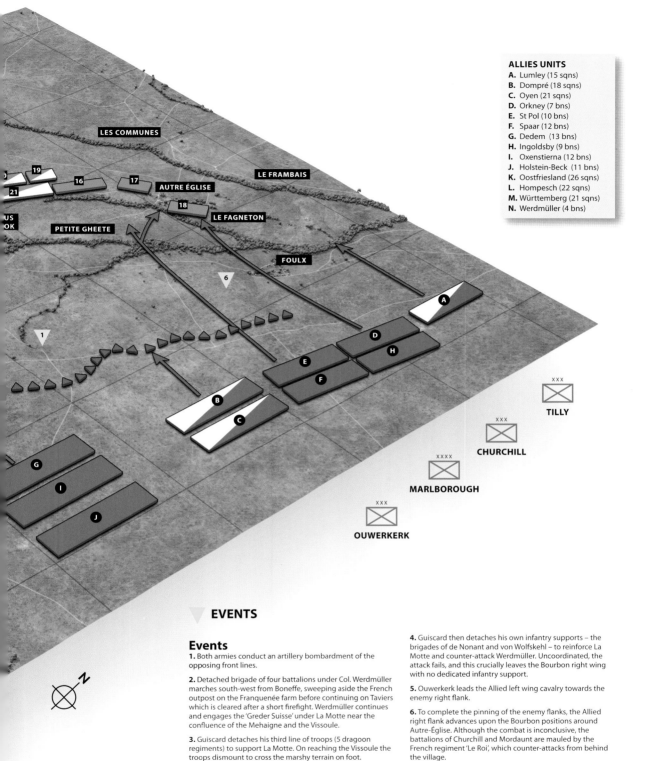

ALLIES UNITS

A. Lumley (15 sqns)
B. Dompré (18 sqns)
C. Oyen (21 sqns)
D. Orkney (7 bns)
E. St Pol (10 bns)
F. Spaar (12 bns)
G. Dedem (13 bns)
H. Ingoldsby (9 bns)
I. Oxenstierna (12 bns)
J. Holstein-Beck (11 bns)
K. Oostfriesland (26 sqns)
L. Hompesch (22 sqns)
M. Württemberg (21 sqns)
N. Werdmüller (4 bns)

▼ EVENTS

Events

1. Both armies conduct an artillery bombardment of the opposing front lines.

2. Detached brigade of four battalions under Col. Werdmüller marches south-west from Boneffe, sweeping aside the French outpost on the Franquenée farm before continuing on Taviers which is cleared after a short firefight. Werdmüller continues and engages the 'Greder Suisse' under La Motte near the confluence of the Mehaigne and the Vissoule.

3. Guiscard detaches his third line of troops (5 dragoon regiments) to support La Motte. On reaching the Vissoule the troops dismount to cross the marshy terrain on foot.

4. Guiscard then detaches his own infantry supports – the brigades of de Nonant and von Wolfskehl – to reinforce La Motte and counter-attack Werdmüller. Uncoordinated, the attack fails, and this crucially leaves the Bourbon right wing with no dedicated infantry support.

5. Ouwerkerk leads the Allied left wing cavalry towards the enemy right flank.

6. To complete the pinning of the enemy flanks, the Allied right flank advances upon the Bourbon positions around Autre-Église. Although the combat is inconclusive, the battalions of Churchill and Mordaunt are mauled by the French regiment 'Le Roi', which counter-attacks from behind the village.

THE OPENING GAMBIT

The opening moves of the battle of Ramillies, which sees the Allied Army under Marlborough attacking the Bourbon flanks in succession in order to prepare for his planned turning manoeuvre and pinning manoeuvre against the enemy right.

third battalion of the Swiss 'Greder' regiment. The remaining companies, under the command of Brigadier La Motte, were engaged some distance to the west in an attempt to destroy the stone bridge across the Vissoule and prevent the enemy from turning the army's extreme right flank. In his own later account La Motte stated his intention to pull his whole command across the waterway and thereby 'place the stream of Tavier, an impassable approach for cavalry, between them and us'. Given that La Motte had, by this early stage of the battle, yet to see an Allied cavalryman, it is clear that his account is more of an attempt to divert royal displeasure rather than an exact account of what had happened. Nonetheless, and reinforced by the dragoon outpost from Franquenée, even with a single battalion, he could easily have brought Taviers into a reasonable state of defence and made the Allies fight for every yard, but the bulk of his troops were too far away from the village and Werdmüller's Dutchmen were soon engaged with the paltry garrison blocking their path.

Once the outer defences had been given up, the succession of walls and hedges soon negated the advantages that Werdmüller derived from his light guns, but the fighting for Taviers was not about tactical finesse, but about using a hammer to crack a walnut. The Swiss held their ground, but not for long, and as the threat of encirclement became a reality, they pulled back from the buildings, hastened by enemy fire, withdrawing to their parent battalion.

In the interim, with the couriers having reached his command position, Guiscard immediately ordered his third line of troops under the Chevalier de Rohan-Chabot to advance as quickly as possible towards Taviers and reinforce the defence of the village or, in the event that it had already fallen, to support a local counter-attack. With five regiments of dragoons, de Rohan spurred forward, even as his commander was taking further action and committed the two brigades of infantry that had been deployed to support the cavalry and act as a rallying point into the attack. Two battalions of French foot – 'Provence' and 'Bassigny' – and three of German troops, the Cologne 'Wolfskehl' battalion and the Bavarian 'Kurprinz' regiment were now soon under way to the crucial sector. A number of commentators have criticized Guiscard and – by extension – Villeroi, for what to modern eyes was a rather haphazard and uncoordinated attempt to stabilize the situation around Taviers. However, the simple fact is that in an era in which battlefield cartography was almost non-existent, to reach a destination that was initially out of sight, the troops would need to move by road; unfortunately, given their initial relative positions, the three formations would be travelling along different routes. In addition, the situation in which La Motte found himself, was unclear indeed.

Looking north towards the site of the cavalry mêlée. The downward slope that gave the French an initial advantage is clearly discernible. (Copyright and courtesy of Seán Ó'Brógáin)

With the Taviers garrison falling back onto his position, La Motte gave up his attempt to destroy the bridge and withdrew westwards onto some rising ground that would give him an advantage against the enemy who, by now, had come through the village and were now re-forming into battle lines to his front.

Advancing to within musket range, Werdmüller gave his men the order to halt and present arms, and then as the company officers began to take over, the sound of discharging muskets began to ripple along the front of his leading battalions, punctuated by the report of the light guns. Atop the hill, the Swiss replied as best they could, but outnumbered and suffering under the relentless, continual discharge of the Dutch platoon fire as casualties mounted, they visibly began to give ground. For almost a quarter of an hour they took this punishment, returning the enemy fire as best they could. Then a runner reached La Motte's position – de Rohan had reached the morass and, having dismounted his troops on the far side, was now hurrying them to his aid, pushing them forward without any consideration of formation or precedence, the sole priority being to shore up the line.

Many dragoons now fell as they rushed into the gauntlet of enemy fire – the Seigneur d'Aubigné was killed at the head of his regiment, whilst both Weißenstein, commander of the Cologne Leibdragoner, and Rohan-Chabot himself had to be dragged to the rear after having been hit by enemy fire. Slowly the Swiss and their reinforcement conceded more ground, but then to the north, the battalions of 'Provence' and 'Bassigny' under the Marquis de Nonant began to arrive – fortuitously enough – behind Werdmüller's right flank, in a position from which they could take the Dutch troops in enfilade. For some minutes it looked as if the tide had at least been halted and the line stabilized, but the French ranks were filled with many for whom this was a baptism of fire and when Werdmüller calmly realigned his flanking battalion to meet the new threat, the newcomers were subject to no less effective a fire as had met 'Greder' at the beginning of the engagement.

The only option was to close with the enemy and, as Nonant attempted to find a way across the morass, he was captured by a party of Dutch troops. Seeing their commander literally *hors de combat*, his brigade withdrew onto the higher ground north of the Vissoule and the opening act of the battle moved inexorably towards its climax with the arrival at the confluence of the German brigade under Wolfskehl. Halting his brigade at the edge of the flooded terrain, the colonel rode forward alone in an attempt to find a route across the waterlogged ground but, as with Nonant, he became bogged down in the marsh and was rescued, but only by the men who would also take him prisoner.

Command now devolved upon a French officer, Lieutenant-Colonel Jean de la Colonie, who was serving as commander of a body of expatriate Frenchmen attached to the 'Kürprinz' regiment. Moving westwards, de la Colonie soon found a route across but disaster struck as he stopped to re-form his troops on the near bank when 'Greder' finally broke in the face of the enemy fire and, dragging the dragoons with it,

Pair of flintlock cavalry pistols made in Vienna by the master gunsmith Simon Penzneter. Weapons of such quality were generally privately purchased and were highly prized owing to their reliability in close combat. (Copyright and courtesy of the Royal Armouries, Leeds)

'CLEARING THE WAY', WEST OF TAVIERS, *c.*1300HRS (PP. 50–51)

Having easily swept aside the Bourbon outposts in Franquenée and Taviers, Werdmüller's ad hoc brigade has continued its advance to the confluence of the Mehaigne and the Vissoule **(1)** only to find its way barred by the remaining companies of the 3rd Battalion of the Greder (Suisse) regiment **(2)** which have deployed on some rising ground shielded by both waterways.

Here, Werdmüller **(3)** is marshalling his forces, the Oranje-Friesland regiment **(4)** engaging the enemy troops to their front whilst the battalions of Salisch and Slangenberg **(5)** repulse a turning movement by which two French infantry regiments – Provence and Bassigny **(6)** – after attempting to enfilade the Dutch line were caught in an unequal firefight and thrown back in disarray, disordering further units that were being rushed

forward to bolster the Bourbon right flank. Behind the rising ground shelter the remnants of Rohan-Chabot's dragoon brigade **(7)** which, having been rushed forward in dismounted order so as to better negotiate the marshy terrain, lost a number of senior officers almost immediately upon coming into action.

By attacking without support and in isolation, the Bourbon commanders were unable to bring their superior numbers to bear and, as such, Werdmüller was able to defeat them in detail and thus facilitate the massing of the Allied cavalry against the Bourbon right flank without any fear of interference from the Mehaigne valley whose occupants were now reduced to the role of spectators as the focus of the combat switched to the north, and the village of Ramillies itself.

fled straight through the newly arrived reinforcements: 'we crossed fairly easily on foot, though in some parts we were over knee-deep in water. Scarcely had my troops gotten over when the dragoons and the Swiss who had preceded us came tumbling down upon my troops in full flight, just at the time as I was re-forming my men after the crossing and a number of my men turned and fled with them.'

The situation was critical as, unbeknownst to Villeroi or even Guiscard, the Bourbon extreme right was teetering on the edge of total collapse, this final reinforcement shattered by the flight of those they had come to support. Standing with a group of bewildered officers, de la Colonie drew his sword and, lashing out at the runaways with the flat of the blade, grabbed hold of the regimental colours and screaming at his men to halt and re-form:

Having passed the Petite Gheete, and then the Fagneton without cavalry support, Orkney's troops would have to face the French troops waiting on the high ground above them. (Copyright and courtesy of Seán Ó'Brógáin)

> I cried out in French and German as if possessed, shouting every epithet I could think of to my grenadiers; I seized the colonel's colour, planted it by me, and by the loudness of my cries I at last attracted the attention of some few of them. The officers who had stood by me rushed after the fugitives, also shouting and pointing to the colonel's colour that I still kept in my hands, and at last they checked the stampede.

Slowly de la Colonie was able to bring order out of the chaos and he cobbled together four small units – in his account of the battle he refers to them as 'battalions' and this is undoubtedly a description of function rather than size – which, taking advantage of the undulating terrain, he pulled back into the protection of some dead ground from where he could observe and, depending on circumstance, interdict the Allied flank attack. Eventually la Motte was also able to rally some survivors and bring them into line behind the German troops, but the damage had been done: Taviers and the road were firmly in enemy hands and, casualties notwithstanding, with the majority of their picketed horses scattered during the flight, Rohan-Chabot's dragoon brigade had ceased to exist as a fighting formation, whilst the remnants of the infantry brigades assigned to support and cover the right-wing cavalry were now reduced to the role of spectators. The door was now open for Marlborough to launch his left wing into the attack.

WHERE THE REDCOATS MARCH

Like the 'sown men' of Thebes, at the shouted order of command, rank upon rank of red-coated infantry rose from the folds of the ground surrounding the hamlet of Foulx. The men had lain there for some hours, resting from the morning's march and sheltering from the impact of cannon balls, which crossed the skies above their heads. It was approaching 2.30pm and their commanding general, George Hamilton, Earl of Orkney, now gave the order for the leading battalions to form up and begin the assault which would secure the villages of Offus and Autre-Église, smashing the enemy's left flank and threatening his line of retreat.

This close-up of one of the tracks leading northwards into Autre-Église clearly shows how the waterlogged fields would have hindered the Allied advance. (Copyright and courtesy of Seán Ó'Brógáin)

This profile image of the terrain north of the Fagneton clearly disproves the impression given in many works that the Bourbon deployment was on relatively flat terrain. (Copyright and courtesy of Seán Ó'Brógáin)

A veteran soldier in every sense of the word, Orkney had used the previous hours to send forward parties of pioneers whose task was to ease the crossing of the Petite Gheete, the first of the watery obstacles his battalions would have to face. With the Communes, Fagneton and Frambais too close to the enemy lines, he knew that the more men he could successfully get across this first hurdle, then the greater would be his chance of successfully achieving his objectives, and in his mind he knew that the French had no troops on the battlefield that could stop his brigades from planting their flags in either of the two villages. Called together by their officers and shoved into position by their NCOs, the scarlet ranks slowly formed – the 1st Battalion, the Foot Guards, whose colonel was the Captain-General, Marlborough himself, the 1st battalion of Orkney's own regiment, then that of the Earl of Stair, more commonly known as the 'Cameronians' and finally those of Godfrey and de Lalo, of Sabine and Webb. And so with their bright colours snapping in the wind, and to the staccato beat of the drum, a line of almost 5,000 men began their march into Villeroi's killing ground.

Across the valley, the French marshal, seeing the enemy advance, nodded knowingly to his staff. The perceived wisdom from Versailles had been that the target of Marlborough's main attack would be where he deployed his own countrymen and the sight of the English battalions moving to threaten the twin villages reaffirmed Villeroi's own belief in the rectitude of his deployment – after all, both settlements were occupied in force and with sufficient supports that could be speedily redeployed in order to deal with any tactical necessity. Slowed down by the marshy terrain, the much-vaunted redcoats would firstly be galled by the musketry of the detachments thrown out to harry their advance and then, disordered and demoralized, they would be shot down before the fortified villages, before being crushed by the Bourbon cavalry coming in from their flank in a scripted victory that would once and for all show that the reputation of Marlborough's infantry was false and inflated.

To Orkney's left stood firstly a brigade of six British battalions under the Irishman George Macartney ('Churchill', 'Mordaunt', 'Evans', 'Macartney', 'Stringer' and 'Howe'), itself flanked by a Danish brigade under Philipp von Donop ('Garde til Fods', 'Prinz Karl', 'Sjaelland' and 'Oldenburg') and as the troops moved forward, the terrain meant that they began to gravitate northwards, imperceptibly opening a gap between themselves and the brigades that were earmarked to assault the enemy centre, the hinge between the formations being covered by Churchill's and Mordaunt's battalions positioned on Macartney's extreme right.

Naturally, modern drainage has had an effect upon the three waterways that the French battalions contested in the face of the Allied advance, but a brief description of one of them as it appears in modern times will serve to give an indication of the obstacles faced by the British troops. The Fagneton is about five feet across, with a depth of about three feet to the waterline which is itself a foot or so in depth, with a muddy bed of several inches. On either side of the stream, the ground slopes down to the bank for a distance of around 50 feet, ground which in May 1706 would have been waterlogged by the previous days' heavy rainfall, the dirt tracks becoming ever more treacherous with the passage of the troops – Orkney himself stated that his brigades took a considerable amount of time to negotiate the obstacles and form up for the attack. In short, it would have been a difficult proposition for an encumbered man to make his way with ease, let alone several thousand attempting to keep formation in the face of a determined enemy defence.

View from Offus looking north-east towards Autre-Église – the position was occupied by a number of Bourbon cavalry brigades who remained largely inactive throughout the battle, their presence dictated by Orkney's movements when they may have been of better use in support of the centre and right flank. (Copyright and courtesy of Seán Ó'Brógáin)

As the three brigades moved off, their place on the heights above Foulx was taken by six battalions ('Ingoldsby', 2nd Bn 'Orkney', 'Farrington', 'Meredith', 'Tatton' and 'Lord North & Grey') under Lt. Gen. Richard Ingoldsby, who held his troops ready to reinforce a successful attack or – in the worst of eventualities – cover a retreat.

Harassed by enemy fire they sprang into the stream bed, using the pioneers' fascines, the dead, the dying and the wounded as stepping stones to continue the advance, with the Bourbon sharpshooters gradually giving way before them as they continued upslope to the next series of obstacles, officers and NCOs pushing them ever forward. Soon both lines of troops became intermingled, the sole objective being to close with the enemy and throw him out of the villages ahead.

Believing that Marlborough was unaware of the tactical situation around Autre-Église, Orkney ignored a series of ADCs sent with instructions for him to withdraw and adopt an offensive posture that would convince Villeroi that the main Allied attack would still fall on his left flank. In exasperation, the Duke finally sent his Quartermaster General, William Cadogan, to ensure that his orders were complied with. At first, Cadogan too, was disbelieved, but eventually Orkney was persuaded to pull his regiments back to their start positions. (Copyright and courtesy of Seán Ó'Brógáin)

Although his unit would not see action until later in the battle, Thomas Kitcher, a member of Meredith's regiment, gives a vivid account of the fighting around Autre-Église. In a memoir that he dictated in later life, he recalled seeing a body being thrown into the stream by pioneers for use as a 'stepping stone', which, having been revived by the cold water after swooning from injuries, sat up and proceeded to let fly a torrent of invective at the hapless soldiers.

Having negotiated the first obstacle under enemy musketry and long-range artillery fire, the Allied troops began to realign their formations for the first phase of Orkney's attack – to seize Autre-Église and then take up a position athwart the Offus–Autre-Église road which would force Villeroi to divert more resources to cover both his open left flank and – just as importantly – his line of retreat towards Louvain.

The attack got into difficulty almost before it started, with the brigades having to constrict their lines and cross on a two-battalion frontage, creating a log jam, which took some time to sort out before the troops could continue their advance. At their head, and disdaining to ride whilst his command marched into the enemy fire, Orkney dismounted and, sword in hand, joined the first of the red-coated ranks to cross the Petite Gheete, urging his men ever onward as they neared the enemy positions. Gradually more and more infantry made it across and the right of the line slowly pivoted towards Autre-Église whilst the left held position on the stream in order to present a forward facing in the event of an enemy counter-attack. At some time between 3.30pm and 4.00pm, Orkney felt that his troops were ready and gave the order for the attack.

Above them, the village garrison – the German musketeers of the Régiment 'Sparre' and their comrades of the Walloon regiments 'Courrières' and 'Zuniga' – confidently poured fire into the Allied ranks but as the enemy numbers increased, they soon found themselves in danger of being outflanked by Churchill's and Mordaunt's Foot who were leading Macartney's brigade. As the redcoats reached the Fagneton, Birkenfeld – a cousin of the Bavarian Elector – in command of the extreme Bourbon left flank ordered the Régiment du Roi forward to plug the gap and in a limited counter-attack – remembered by the modern street known as La Mêlée – the four French battalions threw the two British battalions back before withdrawing uphill once more and adopting a position to screen the south-eastern approach to the village.

For Orkney this was no more than a minor setback; casualties were still light, and he believed that his command still had sufficient numbers and momentum to carry the enemy position and thus facilitate the turning of their flank and so, once again, he exhorted the men around him into another attack. As the English battalions again surged forward, the first of a number of ADCs sent from Marlborough's headquarters arrived on the right flank and, having located the general in the scrum, passed on the Duke's instructions for him to call off the attack and withdraw to his original positions.

There is some dispute in modern accounts about the target of Orkney's attack. Was it the village of Autre-Église? Or was it the village of Offus, which lay at the centre of the Bourbon position, or indeed both? The Earl's own dispatch leaves no room for doubt, when he writes:

Where I was with most of the English foot, there was a morass and *roisseau* before us, which they said was impossible to pass over. But however we tryd, and, after some difficulty, got over with ten or twelve battalions; and Mr Lumley brought over some squadrons of horse with very great difficulty; and I endeavoured to possess myself of a village, which the French brought down a good part of their line to take possession of, and they were on one side of ye village, and I on the other; but they always retired as we advanced. As I was going to take possession, I had ten aid-de-camps to me to come off, for the horse could not sustain me. We had a great deal of fire at this, both musquetry and canon; and indeed I think I never had more shot about my ears; and I confess it vexed me to retire. However we did it very well and in good order, and, whenever the French pressed upon us, with the battalion of guards and my own, I was always able to make them stand and retire.

If we examine the Earl's own words, there are several facts that we can deduce. Firstly, that the initial obstacle his troops had to face was a morass, an area of waterlogged ground, and if we study both the modern 1:50,000 map and the historical map from 1777 provided by Belgium's Institut Géographique National, we can see that the only area along the Petite Gheete to which this description can be applied lies downhill from and directly to the west of Foulx. Secondly, Orkney stated that the enemy 'brought down a good part of their line', which can be seen to describe the advance of the four-battalion Régiment du Roi to support the garrison of Autre-Église and stabilize the left flank, and likewise the Earl's complaint that the enemy continually retired in the face of his advance perfectly describes the harassing fire laid down by the enemy picquets as the British battalions scrambled their way uphill. Thirdly, we have Orkney's own description of how – when he finally acceded to Marlborough's orders to withdraw – he was able to deter the enemy from being too adventurous in any pursuit by redeploying his own regiment's 1st Battalion and that of the Foot Guards, something that would have been relatively straightforward for two veteran and disciplined units if the odds were not stacked too greatly against them. Offus would be attacked but only later during the day; once Autre-Église had already fallen, the Bourbon line had already begun to collapse, and – perhaps most importantly – Henry Lumley had been able to negotiate the Petite Gheete with his mixed brigade of horse and dragoons.

With no sign of Orkney following the instructions that had been relayed by the chain of messengers, Marlborough then sent William Cadogan, his trusted Quartermaster General, to find that officer and ensure his compliance with the commanding general's orders. Many felt that either Marlborough had been misled, that he was ordering the withdrawal without a true appreciation of the situation around Autre-Église, or that Cadogan was simply acting on his own initiative and it was only after a heated discussion that the Earl conceded, giving the orders for his brigades to begin a staged withdrawal to their start lines.

Much ink has been spilled in describing the initial Allied attack on the Bourbon left flank as being a masterstroke of deception that persuaded Villeroi that a tangible threat existed where none existed at all. As G. M. Trevelyan wrote in his three-volume history *England under Queen Anne*:

The manoeuvre of the false attack, by which the enemy was deceived, sounds a simple device. A schoolboy might think of it. But it required a great general and a fine army to carry it out. The honours must be divided between

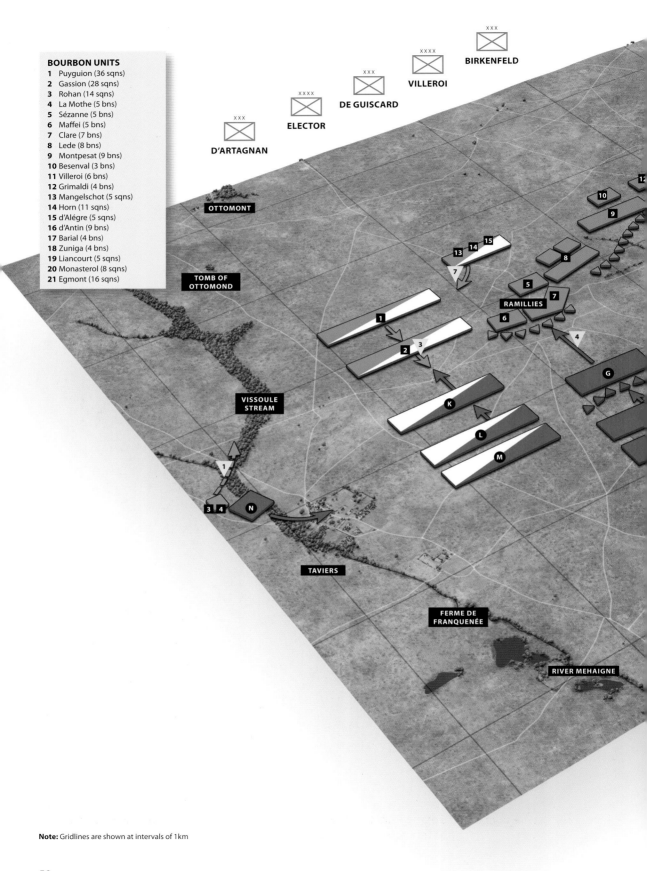

BOURBON UNITS
1   Puyguion (36 sqns)
2   Gassion (28 sqns)
3   Rohan (14 sqns)
4   La Mothe (5 bns)
5   Sézanne (5 bns)
6   Maffei (5 bns)
7   Clare (7 bns)
8   Lede (8 bns)
9   Montpesat (9 bns)
10 Besenval (3 bns)
11 Villeroi (6 bns)
12 Grimaldi (4 bns)
13 Mangelschot (5 sqns)
14 Horn (11 sqns)
15 d'Alégre (5 sqns)
16 d'Antin (9 bns)
17 Barial (4 bns)
18 Zuniga (4 bns)
19 Liancourt (5 sqns)
20 Monasterol (8 sqns)
21 Egmont (16 sqns)

D'ARTAGNAN

ELECTOR

DE GUISCARD

VILLEROI

BIRKENFELD

OTTOMONT

TOMB OF
OTTOMOND

RAMILLIES

VISSOULE
STREAM

TAVIERS

FERME DE
FRANQUENÉE

RIVER MEHAIGNE

Note: Gridlines are shown at intervals of 1km

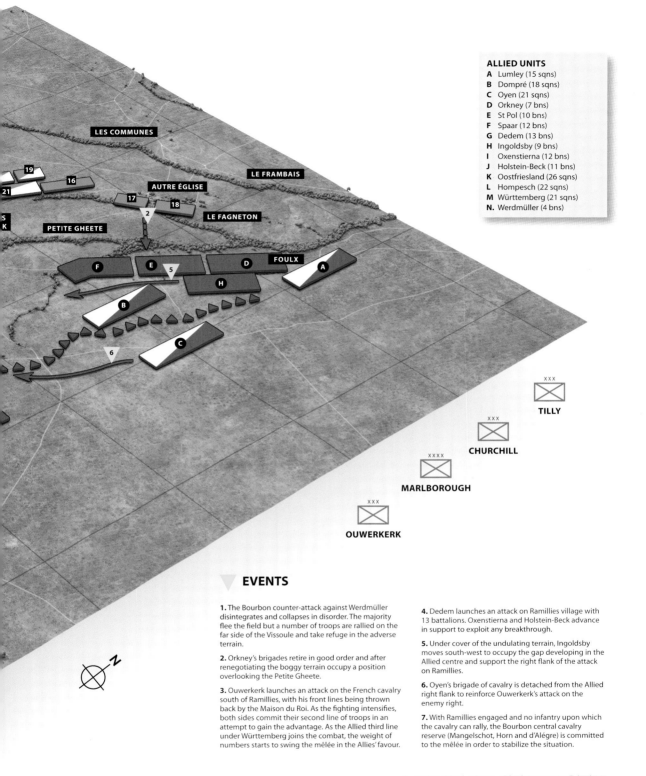

ALLIED UNITS

A Lumley (15 sqns)
B Dompré (18 sqns)
C Oyen (21 sqns)
D Orkney (7 bns)
E St Pol (10 bns)
F Spaar (12 bns)
G Dedem (13 bns)
H Ingoldsby (9 bns)
I Oxenstierna (12 bns)
J Holstein-Beck (11 bns)
K Oostfriesland (26 sqns)
L Hompesch (22 sqns)
M Württemberg (21 sqns)
N. Werdmüller (4 bns)

LES COMMUNES

LE FRAMBAIS

AUTRE ÉGLISE

LE FAGNETON

PETITE GHEETE

FOULX

TILLY

CHURCHILL

MARLBOROUGH

OUWERKERK

▼ EVENTS

1. The Bourbon counter-attack against Werdmüller disintegrates and collapses in disorder. The majority flee the field but a number of troops are rallied on the far side of the Vissoule and take refuge in the adverse terrain.

2. Orkney's brigades retire in good order and after renegotiating the boggy terrain occupy a position overlooking the Petite Gheete.

3. Ouwerkerk launches an attack on the French cavalry south of Ramillies, with his front lines being thrown back by the Maison du Roi. As the fighting intensifies, both sides commit their second line of troops in an attempt to gain the advantage. As the Allied third line under Württemberg joins the combat, the weight of numbers starts to swing the mêlée in the Allies' favour.

4. Dedem launches an attack on Ramillies village with 13 battalions. Oxenstierna and Holstein-Beck advance in support to exploit any breakthrough.

5. Under cover of the undulating terrain, Ingoldsby moves south-west to occupy the gap developing in the Allied centre and support the right flank of the attack on Ramillies.

6. Oyen's brigade of cavalry is detached from the Allied right flank to reinforce Ouwerkerk's attack on the enemy right.

7. With Ramillies engaged and no infantry upon which the cavalry can rally, the Bourbon central cavalry reserve (Mangelschot, Horn and d'Alégre) is committed to the mêlée in order to stabilize the situation.

A TEST OF STRENGTH

Having seized the initiative on his left flank and fixed the enemy's own left flank, Marlborough now launches his planned attack against the Bourbon right and centre, the intent being to secure the village of Ramillies and use it to pivot an attack by Ouwerkerk's cavalry into the enemy rear.

Marlborough and his men. Orkney, in particular must be praised for keeping his head and temper at a moment of confusion, peril and sharp disappointment when some of his subordinates were so angry that they swore Cadogan had invented the orders to retreat.

In a number of accounts we have Orkney's troops re-ascending the slopes towards Foulx with some of their number jeering the French whilst the remainder begin a circuitous march via concealed roads in order to shock the enemy even further by appearing as if from nowhere before joining in the attack on Ramillies itself. But the fact is that Marlborough, having secured Taviers, was now preparing simultaneously to launch the bulk of his cavalry against the Bourbon right flank and columns of infantry against the village of Ramillies.

TO PIERCE THE ENEMY LINE

Having dispatched Cadogan to recall the attack by the right wing, Marlborough now moved his field headquarters south-west, from where he could not only maintain communications with Ouwerkerk, whose cavalry squadrons were by now passing to the south of Ramillies, but also more closely control the Allied infantry columns spearheaded by Karl Wilhelm von Sparre and Willem van Soutlande, which were assembling under cover of the artillery bombardment for an assault on the village.

Under the Captain-General's watchful eye, three infantry brigades – each of six battalions – deployed into three lines of attack: the first brigade, under Major-General Walter Colyear, a Dutch officer of Scottish descent, consisted of one Dutch, one Swedish and two Swiss battalions, supported by two Brandenburg regiments serving on the English establishment; the second brigade, led by the Prussian officer Johann von Ziethen, comprised one Walloon, one Hessian, one Brandenburg and three Hanoverian regiments all in Dutch service; the third assault brigade under Cornelis van Nassau-Woudenburg (*vice* Soutelande) was formed from one Brandenburg, two Swiss and three Dutch battalions. Slightly to the rear, two further brigades stood ready to support the effort – the Dutch Gardes te Voet and the Dutch-Scots Brigade, which consisted of four Scots battalions whose service on the Dutch establishment dated back over four decades. Although other formations were being marshalled into positions from which they could sustain the advance, these units would be the spearhead of the main Allied attack, and their success – or failure – would contribute greatly to the outcome of the battle.

As the infantry mustered, Field Marshal Ouwerkerk began to assemble his own forces for the inevitable combat against the Bourbon cavalry, arrayed slightly to the rear of Ramillies village.

The Chaussée Romaine looking westwards towards the Tomb of Ottomond. Again the rising ground towards the site of the cavalry mêlée can be clearly discerned. (Copyright and courtesy of Seán Ó'Brógáin)

His first line, consisting of 26 cavalry squadrons, was commanded by the 37-year-old Friedrich Ulrich Cirksena, Graaf in Oostfriesland, a veteran officer and cousin of the reigning Count, whose career had been assured when he had saved the life of William III at Neerwinden in 1693. Under his command, Cirksena had three brigades of troops – the first, commanded by Frédéric-Maurice de la Tour d'Auvergne, nephew of the great Turenne, consisted of three regiments of Dutch horse and one of Hanoverian cuirassiers. The second, under Maurits Lodewijk, Graaf van Nassau-La Lecq en Bewerweerd, was made up of four regiments of Dutch horse, whilst the third, led by Daniel Wolfgang, Baron van Dopff, consisted of the cream of the Dutch 'Arme Blanche': two squadrons of the Gardes te Paard and four squadrons each of the Carabiniers and the van Dopff dragoons.

Ouwerkerk's second line was led by Reinhart Vincent, Baron van Hompesch, a 46-year-old officer who had led his troops with great distinction at Blenheim and who had – as a result – become one of Marlborough's most trusted subordinates within the Dutch military hierarchy. Hompesch's command was slightly smaller than that of Cirksena, with three brigades totalling 22 squadrons. The first of these, commanded by Amaury de Farcy, Sieur de St Laurent, a Breton noble who had quit France in 1672 and taken up service with the Duke of Celle, was formed from two regiments of Dutch horse and St Laurent's own regiment of Hanoverians. The second was commanded by the 38-year-old Frederik Sirtema van Grovestins in Westfriesland and comprised four regiments of Dutch horse, whilst the third brigade under Portail contained two regiments of dragoons, each containing four squadrons, from Brandenburg and Holstein-Gottorp respectively.

The third line of the Allied left flank was commanded by Karl Rudolf von Württemberg-Neustadt, a 39-year-old veteran of both the Austro-Turkish Wars, and the Williamite War in Ireland, where he had served under his elder brother Ferdinand Wilhelm as part of the Danish subsidy force and then in the Ukraine where he fought against the Swedes of Charles XII. In similar fashion to the preceding formation, Württemberg's troops were formed into two brigades, each of four regiments of Danish horse, commanded by Johann von Rantzau and Detlev von Brockdorff, respectively, and the five-squadron Württemberg-Oels dragoon regiment under Jakob-Peter von Bonar.

All told, Ouwerkerk now had over half of the army's mounted troops – some 69 squadrons – under his direct command and, from his new command position in the central part of the Allied line, Marlborough gave instructions for Lt. Gen. Matthias Hoeufft, Heer van Oyen, to move with his 21 squadrons of combined horse and dragoons from his position at the rear of the right wing to the left wing, where he would form a fourth rank of cavalry to support Ouwerkerk's attack. The

Possibly the largest cavalry engagement in modern history. This contemporary print evokes the scale and emotion of over 18,000 cavalrymen fighting in the fields south-west of Ramillies village. (Courtesy and copyright of la Bibliothèque Nationale de France)

move would give the Dutchman numerical superiority over his opposite number, the Marquis de Guiscard, but – and this must be stressed – merely parity should the mounted troops held as a central reserve be committed to the Bourbon right flank.

From Marlborough's field headquarters a constant stream of couriers now began to cross the battlefield moving the formations into position and then, as one, the Allied left and centre began their inexorable advance to contact.

A CLASH OF ARMS

Advancing at the walk, Ouwerkerk's horsemen began to veer southwards in order to avoid the enfilade fire that was coming from the southern face of Ramillies, the lines of white- and blue-coated horsemen gradually ascending the heights above the village in order to come to grips with the red-coated troopers impassively waiting for them. And then, at a signal from Guiscard, the chevaliers of France rose to meet the challenge. Spurring their mounts forward, the Maison du Roi – King Louis's household troops, and a microcosm of the French nobility – began to advance, quickly reaching a brisk trot as they moved downhill towards the enemy brigades.

Once the Frenchmen had begun to move from their position, Cirksena gave the signal for his regiments to close up their ranks, his intent being to present the enemy with a single, solid rank of horsemen which would enable him to take advantage of the gaps between the enemy units and, as they gradually began to increase their own speed, the Allied troopers presented a shimmering line of drawn swords, pointing at the advancing foe.

The two lines collided at a fast trot, and initially it seemed as if Cirksena's tactic had backfired, with the first Dutch line thrown back in disorder by the deeper formations of the French Guardsmen, who – in many places – now cut their way through d'Auvergne's brigade and into the regiments of La Leck and Dopff who were advancing to their support. With the elite French cavalry preventing Cirksena's second and third lines from supporting his first, the Prince de Chimay now led a further dozen Franco-Spanish regiments into d'Auvergne's battered troopers, who broke under the pressure and scattered towards the open ground south of Ramillies.

With increasing numbers joining the combat on both sides – historians would later refer to it as the largest cavalry engagement in modern history – the mêlée soon stagnated into a scrum, with the Gendarmerie de la Garde commanded by Henri de Rohan, Prince de Maubuisson, and flanked by the famed *mousquetaires* fighting their way through the Allied lines and into the open ground beyond. Ordering the line regiments of 'Courcillion' and 'Tarente' to use the cover afforded by the fire from Ramillies village and demonstrate against the Allied right, Guiscard left the direction of the combat to Chimay and the Marquis de Puyguion whilst he brought up the regiments of Gassion's second line in order to throw them into the fray, aware that even as he did so, Ouwerkerk was deploying Hompesch's fresh brigades to succour Cirksena's battered troopers and try to regain the initiative on the Allied left, aware that if the reinforcement failed he would be forced to commit Württemberg's Danes, his final reserves before Oyen's brigades had completed their transit from the right flank.

Throughout the morning, Marlborough's artillery had bombarded the enemy lines, and although the Bourbon cannon had reciprocated as best they could, the heavier Allied guns soon began to take their toll on the enemy – an early casualty being the steeple of Ramillies church itself. And now with the cavalry engaged and the infantry columns ready for the assault, the gunfire slackened as the drumbeat intensified signalling the advance.

Sparre's two brigades, under Colyear and Ziethen, stepped off quickly, the troops marching with shouldered arms in order to inhibit the men from firing early and thus reducing the effect of their initial volley. But as they advanced across the fields they soon began to attract the attention of Maffei's Bavarian troops lining the village and were subjected to a largely ineffective fire which served to divert the German battalions' attention from Ouwerkerk's beleaguered troopers, and with the enemy now engaged from the Mehaigne north to Ramillies, Marlborough began to redeploy his formations for the next phase of his plan.

As planned, and preparing to act as a second wave of the attack on Ramillies, Soutelande had deployed his command on a four-brigade frontage, the intent being that the outer formations would effectively flank the village, entering from the north and south, whilst the remaining brigades would pass through Sparre's brigades and defeat an already-exhausted enemy.

Marlborough now brought up two brigades under Bengt Bengtsson Oxenstierna, third son of the Swedish Chancellor, who was to command the column that would push through Ramillies and into the enemy rear. Oxenstierna's first brigade was commanded by Maj. Gen. Steven-Adriaan van Welderen and consisted of one Brandenburg, one Ansbach and four Dutch regiments, whilst the second – two Hanoverian, one Swiss and three Dutch battalions – was led by the Hanoverian Barthold Heinrich von Bernstorff. To complete the move and with Oyen's troopers still en route from the right flank, Marlborough now brought up two further brigades (Keppel and Murray) under the overall command of Anton Günther, Prinz von Holstein-Beck to extend the attack farther to the south, a manoeuvre which would not only return Werdmüller's detachment to its rightful place within the army's command structure, but more importantly provide a solid line of foot, upon which Ouwerkerk could rally his

Having ridden from his command in order to rally a number of broken squadrons that had quit the developing mêlée south of Ramillies, Marlborough soon found himself isolated and the target of a number of French cavalrymen who had cut their way through the Allied horse. As it turned away from the threat, Marlborough's mount lost its footing and threw its rider who hit the ground hard. Momentarily dazed, the Duke cleared his head and got to his feet, running towards the nearest Allied formation – Albemarle's Swiss foot – with the enemy troopers in close pursuit. Thanks to the suppleness of the leather gaiters that he preferred to riding boots, Marlborough was able to run relatively unhindered and luckily reached safety a few strides ahead of his pursuers who were deterred from closing by the steady ranks of Swiss bayonets. (Copyright and courtesy of Seán Ó'Brógáin)

Defended by the Cologne Leibregiment, as the southern part of the Ramillies defences crumbled, the Grande Cense was another substantial farmhouse, the occupation of which by the Bourbons gave the hand-to-hand fighting an almost Vaubanesque quality, in that the Allies could not afford to bypass them. (Copyright and courtesy of Seán of Ó'Brógáin)

cavalrymen, and thereby 'free up' Württemberg's Danish brigades for combat, these units being committed immediately to stabilize the line.

Even as he issued these orders, Marlborough could see that Oyen would arrive far too late to influence the collapse of Ouwerkerk's first line of cavalry and, sending a courier to Nicolaas de Dompré, the Dutch officer commanding the remaining Allied cavalry on the right flank, to bring his command across to support Ouwerkerk, he spurred forward with his headquarters staff in an attempt to rally the fleeing horse, and avert the looming disaster.

Successfully rallying a number of Dutch squadrons, Marlborough led them back into the combat, but in the fluid environment of the cavalry mêlée his suite was scattered when ridden through by other recoiling units and, recognizing the lone red-coated horseman for a senior officer, a group of French cavalrymen gave chase. Dragging his horse's head around, the Duke spurred his mount towards the nearest Allied troops – two battalions of the Swiss regiment 'Albemarle' that held the end of Holstein-Beck's line. As he set his mount against a drainage ditch, the animal baulked and threw its rider, who lay dazed on the ground for several moments and was in danger of being ridden over by a number of Cirksena's men who had by now given up all semblance of order.

Scrambling to his feet, Marlborough began to run towards the Swiss foot, not daring to look behind, and painfully aware that a man on foot was decidedly slower than a man on horse. Seeing his commanding general's predicament, Maj. Gen. Robert Murray ordered his battalions forward at the double, narrowly beating the enemy to the prize, the contest being so close that a number of French troopers, unable to turn their mounts in time, ended up driving them onto the Swiss bayonets.

Newly mounted on a borrowed horse, the Captain-General now began to reassume direction of the battle, when his second charger was brought up by Major James Bringfield of the Life Guards, acting as equerry to the Duke. Alighting from his borrowed mount, Marlborough swung up into his own saddle, and as he did so a round-shot fired from Ramillies passed under his leg and decapitated the unfortunate Bringfield who had been holding the horse steady.

Slowly, superior numbers began to tell and, with neither reserves to sustain them nor a line of infantry supports – these had all been detached to reinforce La Motte at Taviers – behind which they could rally and re-form, the French cavalry began to give ground. The arrival of almost 40 fresh squadrons under Oyen and Dompré tipped the balance, and gradually the exhausted and bloodied Franco-Spanish regiments were forced back uphill, opening up a gap from which the southern approaches to Ramillies could be attacked by the extended line under Holstein-Beck.

THE VILLAGE

The focal point of Marlborough's attack was the small hamlet of Ramillies, a settlement of around 200 people situated on the slopes above the head of the Petite Gheete and which itself – ironically enough given the sustained bombardment that it was about to suffer – was sheltered by a curving ridgeline known locally as the Trou aux Renards: the Foxhole. Typical for the region, the centre of the village was the parish church, a brick-built eminence, surrounded by a gated stone wall, and contemporary maps show us a series of dwellings surrounded by hedged orchards and fields punctuated by two enclosed farms – the Haute Cense and the Basse Cense – both of which are natural defensive positions. Initially, the Bourbon garrison consisted of three battalions of Bavarian troops and two from Cologne, under the Marchese Alessandro de Maffei, a general of Veronese extraction, who had served as the Bavarian second in command at the battle of the Schellenberg in July 1704.

Divining how crucial the defence of the village would be to the integrity of the whole battle line, the Comte d'Artagnan – commanding the Bourbon centre – divided the village into two distinct defensive perimeters and ordered Charles O'Brien, Viscount Clare, to bring forward part of his command to occupy the northern part of Ramillies whilst Maffei's five battalions were to cover the southern sector of the defences and screen the right flank of Guiscard's cavalry brigades. Regrettably we have no concrete narrative of the Bourbon dispositions but, judging from how the fighting for the village would develop, it would seem reasonable to assume that in the south Maffei deployed the three battalions of the Bavarian Leibregiment (two of musketeers and one of grenadiers) together with some light artillery on the south-facing ridge above the Foxhole, whilst the two battalions of the Cologne 'Kurfürst' regiment occupied a perimeter within the village itself. Likewise, and in the other sector, O'Brien deployed the three battalions of the French regiment 'Picardie' in a state of defence whilst his own regiment of Irish émigrés stood ready as an immediate reserve, with a further three battalions of French foot under Albergotti to their rear. With Ramillies now occupied by several thousand infantry supported by a number of artillery batteries, the men now began to prepare in earnest for a protracted defence and even as the Allied cannon fired on the village, roads were being barricaded, buildings loopholed and trenches dug. If the enemy were fated to take Ramillies, d'Artagnan was determined that it would be at great cost.

To the east, Sparre's brigades began their ponderous advance upon the Bourbon strongpoint, the undulating terrain alternately

Charles O'Brien, 5th Viscount Clare (1673–1706). Having gone into exile with the defeated Jacobite forces after the Treaty of Limerick in 1691, O'Brien was appointed colonel of the Queen's Dismounted Dragoons, as part of the Jacobite Army in Exile, serving at Marsaglia in 1693 where his brother the 4th Viscount was killed. In the succeeding years O'Brien served in both Germany and Flanders, participating in all of the major actions, being promoted to brigadier in 1704 and *maréchal de camp* the following year. Commanding the French units defending the centre of the village, O'Brien was wounded several times at Ramillies, refusing all entreaties for him to withdraw from the battle for medical assistance, and he succumbed to his injuries three days after the battle. (Copyright and courtesy of Seán Ó'Brógáin)

View from the Chaussée Romaine looking north-east towards the Allied infantry's line of advance towards Ramillies village. (Copyright and courtesy of Seán Ó'Brógáin)

View of Ramillies village from the Chaussée Romaine. The roof and steeple of the village church can be clearly seen. (Copyright and courtesy of Seán Ó'Brógáin)

concealing and revealing their position, causing the French gunners problems as they tried to find targets in the oncoming ranks. Eventually the Allied foot debouched onto relatively level ground, but their advance ground to a halt in the face of the enemy works as they erupted in a crescendo of gunfire. The Germans, Swiss and Swedes were unable to make much progress as much in the face of the French artillery – which included a number of experimental three-barrelled cannon – as with the implied threat of the Bavarian foot above them and to their flank. Eventually the line thickened as other battalions added their numbers to the front line, and the attacking columns devolved into a reinforced line. For some time the situation remained in a stalemate – the key to the position being the Bavarian battalions dug in on the higher ground whose mere presence prevented the Allied foot from advancing, whilst the flanking elements of the command were able to pour fire into Ouwerkerk's squadrons and disrupt the Allied cavalry in their attempt to overthrow Guiscard's troopers on the Bourbon right flank.

The attack was in danger of grinding to a halt owing to a lack of room to manoeuvre, and as Soutelande's two central brigades halted some distance behind Sparre's men, he threw out his two flanking formations – the Dutch Gardes te Voet and the Dutch Scots Brigade – to extend the line to the south and north of Ramillies respectively in order to stretch the defenders and break the impasse.

Continuing the flanking move, the Dutch guardsmen began to fan out below their Bavarian counterparts and, at the word of command, began a steady advance upslope, pausing only to dress ranks and return the enemy fire that tore into their ranks. Slowly but inexorably the advance continued until, halting one last time, the Blauwe Gardes gave one last volley and then charged the Bavarian works. The attack was never pressed home, as the German foot recoiled and fled downhill to the safety of the village, leaving their dead and wounded as well as their cannon and a number of regimental colours to the victorious Dutchmen. Although inconsequential in the whole drama of the battle, this small local victory was perhaps more than anything else the foundation upon which Marlborough's victory would be built. At a stroke, the pressure on the left-wing cavalry had been removed but, that aside, the Allied foot were now in a position from which they could not only attack the southern approaches to Ramillies, but they could also follow the Foxhole westwards and from there attack the vulnerable and relatively undefended western side of the village.

Likewise, with the central columns needing to regain their cohesion before continuing the attack, the Scots Brigade under the command of the Duke of Argyll – the famed Red John of the Battles – attacked from the north-east, intent on driving towards the village church and splitting the defence. Sword in hand and with Borthwick's regiment in the van, Argyll led his men along the narrow lanes and through the gardens that dotted the village, the other battalions now fanning out to the

An attacker's-eye view: Ramillies as seen from the left flank of Marlborough's attacking columns. (Copyright and courtesy of Seán Ó'Brógáin)

left as the enemy regiments of 'Gondrin' and 'Royal-Italien', the remaining units of Clare's command, were thrown forward to bolster the defences.

Before the red-coated infantry could reach their objective, the church walls erupted with gunfire, the defending musketeers of 'Picardie' signalling that this would be no easy contest for the Scots battalions.

Pausing to take stock of the situation, Colonel William Borthwick saw that the only way successfully to carry the position would be to break into the church precincts, and that to do that he would need to smash down the churchyard gate. A plan was quickly formulated whereby the grenadier company – using their hatchets – would assault the gate, whilst a number of musketeer companies would lay down a suppressing fire and then, once the gate had fallen, the battalion would storm the French position.

Taking a firm hold on the regimental colour, the 19-year-old Ensign James Gardiner waited with the grenadiers and, as the men broke into a run, sprinting for the church wall, he ran with them, the white saltire on blue fluttering defiantly in the wind. Suddenly the young officer was thrown back, dropping the flag as he fell to the ground. A bullet fired from the French position had struck him in the mouth and, spiralling downward, had exited through the back of his neck. Fearing the wound to be fatal, two of the grenadiers took him under his arms and dragged his body to the lee of the wall, where they felt that he could spend his final moments in relative peace.

Gardiner's fall seemed to take the wind out of the Scots' attack, and as

A closer view of Ramillies, as seen from the attackers' perspective. Note that visibility has actually worsened because of the undulating terrain, the ridgeline of the Foxhole being easily made out. (Copyright and courtesy of Seán Ó'Brógáin)

the men re-formed themselves in preparation for another attack, Viscount Clare emerged from one of the side streets and charged into their ranks at the head of his battalion of expatriate Irishmen, all of whom were eager to avenge themselves for the defeats of Aughrim and the Boyne. Amidst a cloud of musket smoke the units mingled with each other, the men laying about each other with musket butt and bayonet. The fact that both regiments wore red coats with yellow facings only added to the confusion, the usual field signs of a white cockade or a sprig of green being largely ignored in the mêlée.

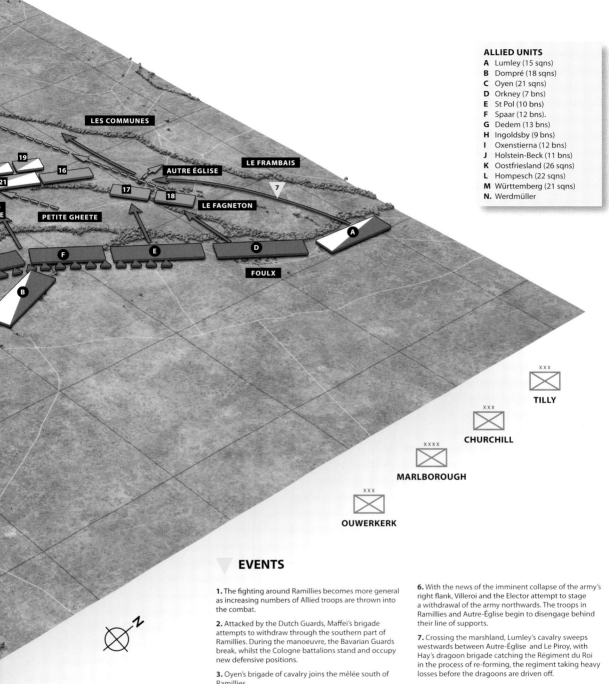

LES COMMUNES

LE FRAMBAIS

AUTRE ÉGLISE

LE FAGNETON

PETITE GHEETE

FOULX

TILLY

CHURCHILL

MARLBOROUGH

OUWERKERK

▼ **EVENTS**

1. The fighting around Ramillies becomes more general as increasing numbers of Allied troops are thrown into the combat.

2. Attacked by the Dutch Guards, Maffei's brigade attempts to withdraw through the southern part of Ramillies. During the manoeuvre, the Bavarian Guards break, whilst the Cologne battalions stand and occupy new defensive positions.

3. Oyen's brigade of cavalry joins the mêlée south of Ramillies.

4. D'Artagnan redeploys his reserve brigades into a new line behind which the Bourbon cavalry can rally.

5. Heavily reinforced by Oyen's brigade, the cavalry mêlée south of Ramillies turns irrevocably in Ouwerkerk's favour and the Bourbon cavalry breaks, fleeing northwards.

6. With the news of the imminent collapse of the army's right flank, Villeroi and the Elector attempt to stage a withdrawal of the army northwards. The troops in Ramillies and Autre-Église begin to disengage behind their line of supports.

7. Crossing the marshland, Lumley's cavalry sweeps westwards between Autre-Église and Le Piroy, with Hay's dragoon brigade catching the Régiment du Roi in the process of re-forming, the regiment taking heavy losses before the dragoons are driven off.

8. With their own cavalry riding through the retreating battalions, the planned withdrawal quickly degenerates into an utter rout.

9. Marlborough orders a 'general advance' and in the ensuing running battle the Bourbon army disintegrates completely and Marlborough achieves his campaign objective of inflicting a major defeat upon the enemy.

A PLAN FULFILLED

Having seized the initiative on his left flank, and fixed the enemy's own left flank Marlborough now launches his planned attack against the Bourbon right and centre, the intent being to secure the village of Ramillies and use it to pivot an attack by Ouwerkerk's cavalry into the enemy rear.

Having by now cut through the leading enemy ranks, the French general was unable to see that his subordinates had indeed followed their orders, but the terrain no longer favoured the necessary cavalry manoeuvres and the commitment of extra troops by both sides became simply an exercise in maintaining pressure on the foe, an exercise in which the commander whose reserves lasted longest would almost certainly emerge the victor. Up until the point that Ouwerkerk was able to commit the Danish cavalry freely, the battle on the Bourbon right hung on a knife edge – with 8,000 of his horsemen engaged against 10,000 of the enemy and, with the continued threat of enfilade fire from the Ramillies defences, it was all that the Dutch commander could do to hold his own and hope to win by attrition, for one enemy regiment to break and recoil, and thereby for the rot to set in. A number of commentators have suggested that, had the Chevalier de Rohan-Chabot been kept in reserve, instead of being committed to the abortive attempt to reinforce Taviers, things could have turned out very differently, but this ignores French tactical doctrine and, in reality, the only mounted troops which could have contributed to the mêlée were the brigades of Beringhen and Costa, at that time deployed in support of d'Artagnan's central position. Although these would have added only some 2,000 sabres to the equation, it would have still given Guiscard numerical parity with his opponent and given him at least a fighting chance of victory.

Forced back by the arrival of Württemberg's Danes, the approach of Oyen's command demonstrated to Guiscard that victory on the right flank was no longer feasible, and he reluctantly gave the order to withdraw back uphill in order to seek a friendly position from where he could rally his battered command. Moving directly away from the enemy threat, the Franco-Spanish cavalry initially headed westwards towards the tumulus known locally as La Tombe d'Ottomond and then, as soon as it was clear that the disengagement had been successful, Guiscard led his racing columns northwards to the centre of the battle line where he hoped to re-form his regiments under the protection of the Marquis d'Artagnan.

From his vantage point above Foulx, Orkney could see the defenders of Autre-Église beginning to leave the village and, rightly discerning that this manoeuvre prefaced a general withdrawal, he gave orders for his command to advance and move against the enemy's line of retreat. Once again the redcoats negotiated the swollen watercourses, but this time they were unopposed and were able to make good progress across the site of the earlier, heavy skirmishing. To their left Lumley's seven regiments of British cavalry also made their way across the Petite Gheete and, with no formed enemy to their front, sought to vent their frustration at their forced inactivity. First blood went to Lord John Hay – second son of the Marquess of Tweeddale – whose brigade, consisting of his own regiment of Scots dragoons and the Irish dragoons of Charles Ross, thundered through the streets of Autre-Église at full gallop. They emerged on the other side, pitching into the battalions of the Régiment du Roi which, in preparation for withdrawal, had moved back to its initial position and where its men were busily collecting the packs and impedimenta that they had discarded before going into action earlier in the day: 'At Ramillies with but three squadrons alone We captured two battalions o' the French "King's Own"; Their blasphemies were awful, but they went their ways in charge o' sax-an'-twenty of the Lord John Hay's, While the rest o'-the lads rode a huntin' the foe a' the moonlit, summer nicht wee big tally-ho.'

Hay's troopers careered into the two rearmost of the French battalions, severely damaging them both and taking many prisoners before being driven off by disciplined volleys from the first and second battalions who, being farther away from the British charge, had been able to take up position in more defensible terrain and redeploy to cover their sister units. Many British commentators would later write of the perfidy of the French soldiers who initially threw their weapons on the ground asking for quarter and after this was given, calmly took up arms again, firing at the men to whom they had so recently given their parole.

The rest of Lumley's command, consisting of five regiments of English horse (Lumley's, Cadogan's, Schomberg's, Wyndham's and Wood's), followed the lesser path driving towards Offus with Orkney's battalions trailing in their wake. Despite a number of clashes with Franco-Bavarian cavalry, which saw Wood's regiment come tantalizingly close to a knot of senior enemy officers who could only have been Villeroi, the Elector and their staffs, and the detritus of combat, which included a large number of cannon, the enemy foot were able to maintain their formation and, without infantry support, Lumley was unable to engage. Again, the Earl of Orkney writes:

I don't know myself what prisoners we have; I am told several major-generalls and others of less note. Lord John Hay's dragoons and others got in upon the Regiment de Roy, which they beat intirely.

There is at least 7 or 800 of 'em prisoners, and everywhere you see colours and standards, and I hear there is at least 40 pieces of canon and a great deal of their baggage. For, whenever they saw that village forced, they immediately retired with such expedition that one could hardly think it possible. We pursued them till dark night, but their horse it was impossible to get at. Their foot Mr Lumley with severall English squadrons came nigh, but without foot it was impossible to attack them. He sent to me that, if I could come up with

'ENEMY AT BAY', WEST OF AUTRE-ÉGLISE, *c.*1800HRS (PP. 84–85)

With the Allied forces closing with the enemy all along the front line Lt. Gen. Lumley's cavalry, on the Allied right, begins to negotiate its way across the Petite Gheete and the marshy terrain to the south and east of Autre-Église and, finding the village deserted, the frustrated troopers gallop westwards in an attempt to find and engage the enemy before the fighting draws to a close.

Thundering through a line of trees, Lord John Hay at the head of his own regiment of dragoons **(1)** – later the Scots Greys – and that of Charles Ross **(2)** – later the Royal Irish – bursts out into the midst of two battalions of the French Régiment du Roi **(3)** who are in the process of gathering their packs and knapsacks **(4)** discarded prior to being sent into action around Autre-Église.

Although small knots of men try to rally and hold off the marauding horsemen, many **(5)** simply turn and flee towards the other two battalions of the regiment which have formed up and present a line of loaded muskets at the British horsemen.

Nevertheless the damage has been done – the French regiment has been shattered, suffering a reputed 800 casualties, and now the remainder of Lumley's command ranges over the northern sector of the battlefield, their presence hastening the disintegration of Villeroi's planned withdrawal into an uncontrolled rout.

the foot, he did not doubt but we would take eight or nine batallions of 'em that were in a body together. I marched I am sure as fast as it was possible for men to march, and ordered them to lose no time, and that I would ride up to Mr Lumley myself. I own it vexed me to see a great body of 'em going off, and not many horse with them; but, for my heart, I could not get up our foot in time; and they dispersed and got into strong ground where it was impossible to follow them.

To the south, d'Artagnan's beleaguered battalions were being squeezed out of the northern outskirts of Ramillies, their position being threatened by the inexorable Allied advance. The exhausted general attempted to keep order as best he could, basing his formation around the large French regiments of 'Alsace' and 'Picardie', which between them still numbered over 4,000 effectives, and Clare's Irishmen, who still carried their mortally wounded commander within their ranks, refusing to leave him to the care of the enemy. But with lesser regiments now disintegrating and sowing the first seeds of a total collapse of discipline, even these units began to feel the mounting pressure, their officers unable to be everywhere at once.

Retreating gradually and harried by the enemy every step of the way, the Frenchmen buckled on a number of occasions but, refusing to break, continued towards the line of troops at Offus, whose glittering muskets seemed to promise a release from the stinging enemy attacks. Shielded by the guards brigade to the east, the blasted remnants of the Bourbon centre were now ordered to take position behind the regiments of 'La Marck' and 'Montroux', of 'Isenghien' and 'St Sulpice', all yet to fire a shot in anger but,

Although modern research has shown that the Bourbon collapse was not as total as initially believed, this contemporary print evocatively conveys the image of an army on the brink of disaster. (Courtesy and copyright of la Bibliothèque Nationale de France)

once a retrograde movement begins, it is often difficult to stop and so was the case here. Realizing that there was no real possibility of his army being able to conduct a fighting retreat, Villeroi gave orders for a general disengagement, by which the various formations would attempt to quit the field as best they could and ultimately aim to re-form at Tirlemont on the Dyle.

That should have been the end of the battle, with the Bourbon forces conceding defeat – and the field – to the Allies, and so it should have been, at least to the retreating generals' way of thinking. However, Villeroi had never commanded in the field against Marlborough and therefore lacked the

The memorial plaque for the tercentenary of the battle of Ramillies that was unveiled on the battlefield following the 2006 celebrations. (Copyright and courtesy of Seán Ó'Brógáin)

appreciation of his opponent's determination to win the war by smashing his opponent's ability to wage further hostilities. He was thus totally wrong-footed when the Duke released his army in a general chase, in an attempt to cause as much physical and logistical damage to the enemy as possible before darkness fell. But this final attack should not be simply seen as the final 'bludgeoning' of a beaten enemy, for Marlborough was aware of one crucial factor that would determine not only the closing moments of the battle but also the 1706 campaign as a whole. This was simply that, in order to fill the ranks of his army with Allied Spanish forces, Villeroi had stripped many of Flanders' fortresses totally bare of defenders and, thus, the key to many of these fortresses now lay in front of the Allied troops; all Marlborough had to do was to reach out and grab it.

With the Allied left and right wings now closing in on each other, the trap was almost complete and it was inevitable that cries of 'sauve qui peut' – let he save himself who can – began to be heard rising from the Franco-Spanish ranks. And whilst many Allied soldiers broke ranks to loot the enemy encampment and baggage train, many more were kept in hand to continue the bloody pursuit, smashing the remnants of Villeroi's proud army as, depending upon the regiment and corps, they either fled in disorder or marched purposefully northwards, determined to reach the army's rallying point at Tirlemont, their commanders unaware, as darkness fell, of exactly how dangerously dispersed Marlborough's cavalrymen had become during the pursuit, being more than grateful to put the river between them and their enemy, hopeful of using the hours of night and the early morning dawn to try to salvage some order from the debacle.

THE AFTERMATH

In terms of casualties inflicted upon the Bourbon Army, the magnitude of Marlborough's victory remains difficult to quantify. John Millner, who served under the Duke, suggests that Villeroi lost 12,087 dead and wounded with a further 9,729 being taken as prisoners, a figure that is similar to the 20,000 casualties cited by Voltaire. In 1872, Capitaine Marchal quoted a total figure of 13,000 casualties, together with 80 standards, almost all of the artillery and all of the baggage. In more modern works, Chandler cites 12,000 dead and wounded with 7,000 prisoners; Falkner concurs with Chandler's estimate of the casualties but increases the number of prisoners to around 10,000; whilst Litten, citing French archives, suggests that the French contingent alone lost some 7,000 dead and wounded with around 6,000 being taken prisoner, whilst a possible further 2,000, having decided that 'discretion is the better part of valour', simply used the confusion as an opportunity to desert the colours.

'The Year of Miracles'. This 19th-century German postcard shows Prince Leopold von Anhalt-Dessau leading Prussian troops into action against the French regiment 'La Marine' at Turin on 7 September 1706. Having run out of ammunition the Frenchmen were unable to resist the Prussian attack, and Dessau smashed the Bourbon right flank, securing victory and relieving the three-month siege of the city. (Author's collection)

In any event, the loss of a possible 20,000 men from an army that had earlier mustered some 60,000 effectives can be referred to only as a disaster, and it would soon be viewed as such at Versailles, as many officers lost no time in writing to their patrons and superiors at Court to exonerate their conduct and damn their peers. But the true scale of the defeat would be illustrated firstly by the fact that, after Ramillies, the Spanish Army of Flanders, and the Bavarian and Cologne 'armies in exile' simply ceased to exist, and secondly by the fact that, in so mustering his troops that he could achieve numerical parity with Marlborough, Villeroi had stripped the garrisons of a number of strategically important fortresses, down to almost criminal levels. Thus, whilst the remnants of the Bourbon field army withdrew northwards and then westwards, Marlborough was able to exploit the enemy's collapse to the fullest.

With Villeroi and the Elector falling back on Ghent and without needing to wait for the siege train to be brought up, Marlborough followed in their wake and, after crossing the Dyle, took Louvain on 25 May. Brussels followed suit two days later and as the army continued its advance, detachments were sent out to summons a number of strategically important towns and cities, perhaps the most significant of which was Antwerp, which surrendered to Cadogan on 5 June, and the bulk of whose predominantly Spanish garrison promptly enlisted in the army of King Charles III. By mid-month there was a very real danger that much of the army might have to be put into garrison in order to maintain the Allied hold on all that had fallen to them in the aftermath of the battle.

Elsewhere, the Allies reported success after success. In Spain, the Bourbons were forced to abandon their siege of Barcelona on 27 April, whilst in Northern Italy, Vendôme was recalled and sent to Flanders in order to shore up the disastrous situation, his place being taken by the Duc d'Orléans and the Marquis de la Feuillade who proceeded to besiege the city of Turin with an army of over 40,000 men. It looked as if the Savoyard capital was doomed, but then on 7 September, Eugène attacked the siege lines with a smaller force and, despite being repulsed three times, the re-formed Prussian corps of Leopold von Anhalt-Dessau smashed through the French lines and scattered the besiegers, one notable casualty being Marshal Marsin who was serving as an adviser to Orléans.

For the Allies, and despite Villars's continued successes on the Rhine frontier, 1706 had proven to be an *annus mirabilis* – a year of miracles – the unprecedented, and in some quarters unanticipated, successes of which boded well for a successful conclusion to the war. It was an understandable optimism, but one which would prove to be unfounded as negotiations foundered in the face of the entrenchment of a number of the principals and the conflict would continue for another eight years.

The aftermath

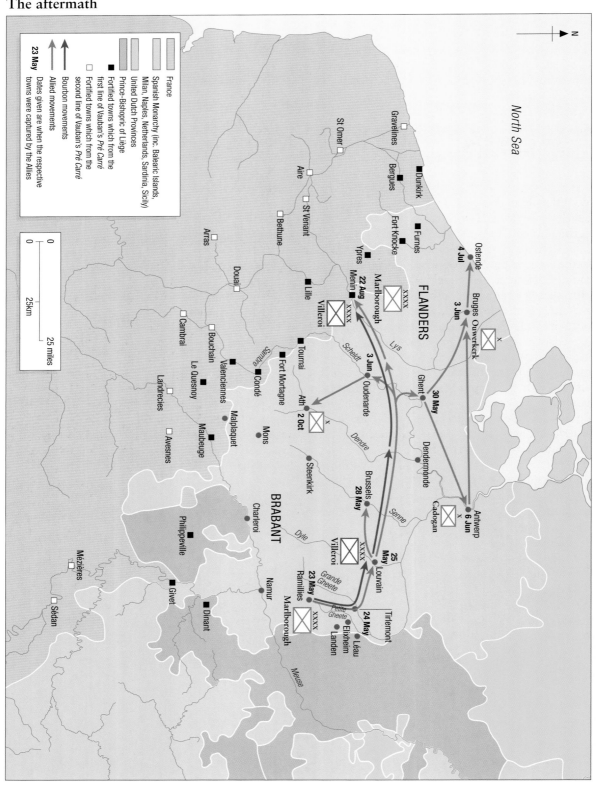

THE BATTLEFIELD TODAY

With the obvious exception of the villages themselves, which have grown and developed over the last three centuries, and the waterways, which have been drained to suit local needs, much of the battlefield remains as it was in May 1706. Thanks to the many local roads, much of the battlefield is accessible to the visitor and the NGI 1:50,000 scale map for Wavre is an indispensable tool for planning a battlefield trip, which can be accomplished in a single day. However, the author recommends that a two- or three-day visit would enable a more relaxed excursion, with the added option of following in the tracks of each of the combatant armies as they made their way to the battlefield.

As for accommodation, with the battlefield situated almost equidistant between the cities of Brussels, Louvain and Namur, each of which has its own historical attractions, the visitor is relatively spoilt by an excess of riches, although for the purposes of researching this book the author and photographer stayed at, and at the pension Au Temps de Cerises in Autre-Église (www.autempsdecerises.be) which is situated on the Rue Armand Guerlache, near to 'La Mêlée' where the Régiment du Roi and Churchill's–Mordaunt's regiments met in the initial combat.

Until the 2006 tercentenary of the battle, this small roadside chapel that lies on the Rue de Fodia – astride the Allies' attack routes to Ramillies, Offus and Autre-Église – was the sole monument to a battle which almost ended the War of the Spanish Succession. (Photo and copyright Seán Ó Brógaín)

FURTHER READING

Belloc, Hilaire, *Six British Battles*, J.W. Arrowsmith, Bristol, 1931

Bernier, Olivier, *Louis XIV – A Royal Life*, Doubleday, New York, 1987

Bredin, Brigadier A. E. C., *A History of the Irish Soldier*, Century Books, Belfast, 1987

Bureau de la Guerre, *Chronologie Historique Militaire de la France* (8 vols), Paris, 1860

Churchill, Winston S., *Marlborough, His Life and Times*, Charles Scribner's Sons, New York, 1966

Courcelles, Chevalier de, *Dictionnaire Historique et Biographique des Généraux Français depuis le 11e siècle jusqu'au 1820* (9 vols), Paris, 1820

Crichton, Andrew, *Life & Diary of Lt. Col. J. Blackader*, London, 1824

Dalton, John, *English Army Lists and Commission Registers: 1661–1714* (6 vols) – Vols V/VI, Francis Edwards, London, 1960

Fricke, Gustav, *Der Bayerische FM Alessandro Marchese Maffei*, Berlin, 1891

Golberg, Claus-Peter and Hall, Robert, *The Army of the Electorate Palatine under Elector Johann-Wilhelm, 1690–1716*, Pike and Shot Society, Farnham, 2004

Hall, Robert, *Flags and Uniforms of the French Infantry under Louis XIV, 1688–1714*, Pike and Shot Society, Farnham, 2004

——, *The Armies of Hesse and the Upper Rhine Circle*, Pike and Shot Society, Farnham, 2007

Hall, Robert and Boeri, Giancarlo, *Uniforms and Flags of the Imperial Austrian Army 1683–1720*, Pike and Shot Society, Farnham, 2009

Hall, Robert, Boeri, Giancarlo and Roumegoux, Yves, *Guidons, Flags and Uniforms of the French Dragoons, Militia, Artillery and Bombardiers under Louis XIV, 1688–1714*, Pike and Shot Society, Farnham, 2003

Hall, Robert, Boeri, Giancarlo and Roumegoux, Yves, *Standards and Uniforms of the French Cavalry under Louis XIV, 1688–1714*, Pike and Shot Society, Farnham, 2005

Holmes, Richard, *Marlborough, England's Fragile Genius*, Harper Collins, London, 2008

Hugill, J. A. C., *No Peace without Spain*, Kensal Press, Oxford, 1991

Kane, Richard, *Campaigns of King William and Queen Anne*, London 1745

Lecestre, Léon, *Mémoires du Chevalier de Quincy* (3 vols), Paris, 1898

Lossky, Andrew, *Louis XIV and the French Monarchy*, Rutgers University Press, New Jersey, 1999

Lynn, John A., *Giant of the Grand Siècle: The French Army 1610–1715*, Cambridge University Press, New York, 1998

——, *The Wars of Louis XIV, 1667–1714*, Longman, Harlow, 1999

Marchal, Capitaine, *Abrégé des Guerres de Louis XIV*, Louvain, 1872

Moret, Ernest, *Quinze Ans du Règne de Louis XIV, 1700–15*, 3 vols, Paris, 1859

Nosworthy, Brent, *Anatomy of Victory: Battle Tactics 1689–1763*, Hippocrene Books, New York, 1992

O'Callaghan, John Cornelius, *History of the Irish Brigades in the Service of France*, Irish University Press, Shannon, 1968

Ó Ciardha, Éamonn, *Ireland and the Jacobite Cause, 1685–1766: A Fatal Attachment*, Four Courts Press, Dublin, 2002

Petrie, Sir Charles, *The Marshal Duke of Berwick*, Eyre and Spottiswoode, London, 1953

Pevitt, Christine, *The Man Who Would Be King – The Life of Philippe d'Orléans, Regent of France*, Weidenfeld and Nicolson, London, 1997

Rowlands, Guy, *The Dynastic State and the Army under Louis XIV: Royal Service and Private Interest, 1661–1701*, Cambridge University Press, Cambridge, 2002

Taylor, Frank, *The Wars of Marlborough* (2 vols), Basil Blackwell, Oxford, 1921

Trevelyan, G.M., *England under Queen Anne* (3 vols), Longmans, London, 1948

Walton, Col. Clifford, *History of the British Standing Army, 1661–1700*, Harrison & Sons, London, 1894

Weber, Arnold, *Biographisches Lexikon aller Helden und Militärpersonen welche sich im Preußischen Dienst berühmt gemacht haben* (3 vols), Berlin, 1788

White-Spunner, Barney, *Horse Guards*, Macmillan, London, 2006

Wolf, John B., *Louis XIV*, Victor Gollancz, London, 1968

INDEX